ALMOST ANXIOUS

ALMOST ANXIOUS

Is My (or My Loved One's) Worry or Distress a Problem?

Luana Marques, PhD, Harvard Medical School

with Eric Metcalf, MPH

HAZELDEN®

Hazelden
Center City, Minnesota 55012
hazelden.org

Library of Congress Cataloging-in-Publication Data

Marques, Luana.
    Almost anxious : is my (or my loved one's) worry or distress a problem? / Luana
Marques, PhD, Harvard Medical School, with Eric Metcalf, MPH.
       pages cm
Includes bibliographical references.
    ISBN 978-1-61649-447-6 (pbk) — ISBN 978-1-61649-469-8 (ebook)
1. Anxiety. 2. Anxiety disorders. 3. Worry.
I. Metcalf, Eric. II. Title.
    RC531.M35 2013
    616.85'22—dc23
                                                                        2013021530

Editor's notes:
The case examples in this book are composite examples based upon behaviors
encountered in the author's own professional experience. None of the individuals
described in this book are based on a specific patient, and all identifying details in
the composite examples have been changed to protect the privacy of the people
involved.

    This publication is not intended as a substitute for the advice of health care
professionals.

17 16 15 14 13   1 2 3 4 5 6

Cover design by Theresa Jaeger Gedig
Interior design and typesetting by Kinne Design

Harvard Health Publications
HARVARD MEDICAL SCHOOL
Trusted advice for a healthier life

The Almost Effect™ **series** presents books written
by Harvard Medical School faculty and other
experts who offer guidance on common behavioral
and physical problems falling in the spectrum between
normal health and a full-blown medical condition.
These are the first publications to help general readers
recognize and address these problems.

❖

For Dona Maria Helena Esteves Martins—

my first psychology mentor

contents

List of Figures

List of Exercises

The Almost Effect

I once overheard a mother counseling her grown daughter to avoid dating a man she thought had a drinking problem. The daughter said, "Mom, he's not an alcoholic!" The mother quickly responded, "Well, maybe not, but he *almost* is."

Perhaps you've heard someone, referring to a boss or public figure, say, "I don't like that guy. He's *almost* a psychopath!"

Over the years, I've heard many variations on this theme. The medical literature currently recognizes many problems or syndromes that don't quite meet the standard definition of a medical condition. Although the medical literature has many examples of these syndromes, they are often not well known (except by doctors specializing in that particular area of medicine) or well described (except in highly technical medical research articles). They are what medical professionals often refer to as subclinical and, using the common parlance from the examples above, what we're calling *the almost effect*.

For example:

- Glucose intolerance may or may not always lead to the medical condition of diabetes, but it nonetheless increases your risk of getting diabetes—which then increases your risk of heart attacks, strokes, and many other illnesses.

- Sunburns, especially severe ones, may not always lead to skin cancer, but they always increase your risk of skin cancer, cause immediate pain, and may cause permanent cosmetic issues.

- Pre-hypertension may not always lead to hypertension (high blood pressure), but it increases your risk of getting hypertension, which then increases your risk of heart attacks, strokes, and other illnesses.

- Osteopenia signifies a minor loss of bone that may not always lead to the more significant bone loss called osteoporosis, but it still increases your risk of getting osteoporosis, which then increases your risk of having a pathologic fracture.

Diseases can develop slowly, producing milder symptoms for years before they become full-blown. If you recognize them early, before they become fully developed, and take relatively simple actions, you have a good chance of preventing them from turning into the full-blown disorder. In many instances there are steps you can try at home on your own; this is especially true with the mental and behavioral health disorders.

So, what exactly is the almost effect and why this book? *Almost Anxious* is one of a series of books by faculty members from Harvard Medical School and other experts. These books are the first to describe in everyday language how to recognize and what to do about some of the most common behavioral and emotional problems that fall within the continuum between normal and full-blown pathology. Since this concept is new and still evolving, we're proposing a new term, *the almost effect*, to describe problems characterized by the following criteria.

The problem

1. falls outside of normal behavior but falls short of meeting the criteria for a particular diagnosis (such as alcoholism, major depression, psychopathy, anorexia nervosa, or substance dependence);

2. is currently causing identifiable issues for individuals and/or others in their lives;

3. may progress to the full-blown condition, meeting accepted diagnostic criteria, but even if it doesn't, still can cause significant suffering;

4. should respond to appropriate interventions when accurately identified.

The Almost Effect

All of the books in The Almost Effect™ series make a simple point: Each of these conditions occurs along a spectrum, with normal health and behavior at one end, and the full-blown disorder at the other. Between these two extremes is where the almost effect lies. It is the point at which a person is experiencing real pain and suffering from a condition for which there are solutions—*if* the problem is recognized.

Recognizing the almost effect not only helps a person address real issues now; it also opens the door for change well in advance of the point at which the problem becomes severe. In short, recognizing the almost effect has two primary goals: (1) to alleviate pain and suffering now, and (2) to prevent more serious problems later.

I am convinced these problems are causing tremendous suffering, and it is my hope that the science-based information in these books can help alleviate this suffering. Readers can find help in the practical self-assessments and advice offered here, and the current research and clinical expertise presented in the series can open opportunities for health care professionals to intervene more effectively.

I hope you find this book helpful. For information about other books in this series, visit www.TheAlmostEffect.com.

Julie Silver, MD
Associate Professor, Harvard Medical School
Chief Editor of Books, Harvard Health Publications

acknowledgments

It takes a village to raise a child, and this book would not have been birthed without the continuous support of my own tribe. I would like to first thank Eric Metcalf, MPH, for your editorial support; without your writing suggestions, this book would have been another "boring" academic paper. I would also like to thank Julie Silver, MD, and Sid Farrar for your editorial guidance and support, and Nicole LeBlanc, Ann Elizabeth Yacoubian, and Louise E. Dixon for your research assistance. This book would surely not exist without your invaluable support, enthusiasm, and continuous motivation. Thanks also to the great staff at both Harvard Health Publications and Hazelden. And to Linda Konner, literary agent for The Almost Effect™ series, I appreciate you making this book a reality.

To all of the experts who reviewed book chapters, I can't thank you enough for sharing your clinical, personal, and research insights. Your feedback ensured the quality of this book: Jennifer J. Thomas, PhD; Juliana Belo Diniz, MD; John J. Worthington, MD; Donald J. Robinaugh, MA; Diana Higgins, PhD; Sarah K. Franco; Lois Hayes; Laurel Blackford de Zepeda; and Steffany J. Fredman, PhD. I can't thank you enough for your comments on previous drafts of this manuscript. I would also like to recognize David Zepeda,

PhD, whose artistic abilities "surpassed" his business doctoral degree. David, your steady instrumental and emotional support ensured the timely delivery of this manuscript.

To my family and friends, I could not have finished this book without you. I would like to specially thank my mother, Bel Marques, for your unconditional love and dedication. I am also very grateful to my stepfather, Luiz Fernando Esteves Martins, for your unwavering support and guidance. I also would like to recognize the support of my sister and my father, Juliana Marques Elias and Almir de Oliveira Junior. I would not have become a clinical psychologist without the mentorship and guidance of my dear friend Susan A. Gunn. I would also like to express my deepest gratitude to the Hayes family for welcoming me into their family and thus allowing me to pursue the American dream. Finally, to many of my personal friends—you know who you are—thank you for the tender love and care that you have given me during the last year while I wrote this book. Your generosity, care, and attention haven't gone unnoticed.

I would also like to thank the organizations that have generously funded my scientific research, including the National Institute of Mental Health (NIMH) and the Multicultural Affairs Office at Massachusetts General Hospital (MGH). I would also like to acknowledge my amazing colleagues at the Center for Anxiety and Traumatic Stress Disorders at MGH, with a special thanks to Dr. Naomi Simon for providing continuous mentorship and ensuring my academic progress, as well as my colleagues at the MGH-Chelsea Mental Health clinic, especially Dr. Mary Lyons-Hunter and Marie Deloreto. I also would like to recognize the chief of psychiatry at MGH,

Jerrold F. Rosenbaum, MD, for his ongoing support and professional guidance. Finally, I want to wholeheartedly thank all of the patients who have entrusted me with their emotional care. You have taught me the most about almost anxiety. Because of your stories and trust, this book exists.

■ ◆ ■

Even a *Little* Too Much Anxiety Is a Problem Worth Solving

In my line of work, I see anxiety of all flavors and intensity. I'm an assistant professor at Harvard Medical School and a licensed clinical psychologist in the department of psychiatry at Massachusetts General Hospital in Boston.

Every single day, people come into my office to talk with me about their anxiety. My patients—who are mostly adults—come from all walks of life, from the high-powered attorney who has trouble focusing at work to the single parent who lies awake at night worrying about unpaid bills. Some have a little anxiety. Some have lots. Many fall somewhere in between.

For some of my patients, worrisome thoughts merely intrude into their minds more than they'd like. Their fears and doubts are just distracting and unpleasant enough to spur them to come see me for help in managing the occasional upheaval in their lives.

For others, anxiety completely prevents them from enjoying any peace and normalcy. It has damaged their relationships. It has interfered with their ability to succeed at work. At the extreme end, anxiety prevents some from leaving their homes or speaking to other people, resulting in a very isolated life.

Young, old, rich, or poor, the common denominator among the folks I see is this: "I have too much anxiety."

This consistent theme raises the question: What is too much anxiety? Should you strive to be rid of *all* anxiety in your life? No! That's not realistic, nor is it the goal of this book. Having *some* anxiety isn't a bad thing. In fact, a little anxiety can propel you through a happy, successful life, much like a motor on a boat. Having too much anxiety, however, is a bad thing—even if it's just a *little* too much.

Like many others, you might also live under the assumption that people either have a problem with anxiety or they don't. This is not surprising given that many doctors and scientists share this perspective of anxiety as a dichotomous category, meaning that someone is either normal or has a diagnosable anxiety disorder. If we were to draw a picture of this view, it would look like figure 1.

Figure 1.
Either Normal or a Disorder

Normal Mood	Anxiety Disorder

Through my clinical and research work with anxiety disorders, I have grappled with this issue and arrived at the concept of being *almost anxious*. Being "almost" anxious is an unfamiliar concept to many of the patients I see. It may feel new to you too.

Here's what it means to be almost anxious: it's having a sense of anxiety that persistently reduces your quality of life. The nagging, worrisome thoughts in your mind distract you from the positive, enjoyable experiences all around you. Being almost anxious keeps you from approaching new experiences in life, and it limits your ability to pursue your interests. This, in turn, drags down your quality of life and well-being.

On the other hand, although it's making your life unpleasant, almost anxiety (another term I use for being almost anxious) isn't so profound that a psychiatrist, psychologist, or other mental health worker would diagnose you with—or treat you for—a full-fledged anxiety disorder. That's where the "almost" comes in.

One way to understand being almost anxious is to look at an example of a real-life person who was feeling this way. Here's the story of one of my patients who I'll call Mark. (All of the case examples in this book, by the way, are composites based on people I've encountered in my own professional experience. None of the individuals you'll meet in these pages are actual patients. All names and details have been changed to protect the privacy of the people involved.)

Mark's Story

Mark was a highly educated and successful thirty-five-year-old. He was doing well at his job as a business manager in a large company in the Midwest, with several recent promotions and a team of twenty employees working under him. Even so, he told me that he "just could not stop worrying." Mark felt a constant sense of doom, often fretting that a mistake at work could cost him his job. He said he had always been a worrier, but his thoughts had never bothered him until three months earlier.

At that time, he was promoted to his current management position, and he immediately started having trouble sleeping. He began to feel edgy and preoccupied. And he became unable to stop his mind from racing and worrying. All of these concerns started affecting his life. He could no longer concentrate fully, which caused him to stay longer at work to finish his tasks, ultimately resulting in difficulties with his girlfriend. She began complaining that she didn't see Mark enough.

"At night, my mind races, thinking of all the things I have to do tomorrow and all of the possible things that might go wrong. I wonder about how my meetings will turn out and if I will be able to handle the pressures of the day. I find myself lying in bed for hours trying to calm down. I am just too anxious to sleep," he told me. Mark had finally decided to come see me because he realized that his worries were interfering with his life.

At first glance, it appeared that Mark's turmoil was related to his job promotion and that after adapting to his new role, he might be able to decrease his anxiety. Yet as we talked more, Mark revealed that even though his worries had never bothered him before, he had *always* experienced a low level of worry. He remembered being concerned that he might fail tests in college, even though he had always been a good student. Thus, he often found himself studying longer than was really necessary. Thinking back, Mark said he wished he had attended a few more parties in college or dated more instead of "excessively" studying to manage his worries.

Mark is a great example of someone who is almost anxious. He has some of the characteristics of generalized anxiety disorder (GAD), a full-fledged psychiatric condition in which the person feels a *nearly constant* sense of anxiety and worry that *significantly* interferes with *many* areas of his or her life.

If we view anxiety as occurring along a spectrum, as in figure 2, we can see that Mark would fall between normal levels of anxiety and disordered anxiety.

Figure 2.
The Anxiety Spectrum

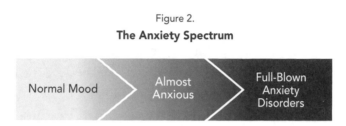

However, when I met with him, Mark's emotional difficulties would not meet the criteria for any of the anxiety disorder diagnoses. For starters, his worry level had only been bothersome for the past three months, which is three months shorter than the required timeline for the diagnosis of GAD. Additionally, Mark did not have some of the other symptoms associated with GAD, such as restlessness and muscle tension.

Even though his worries were not rising to a clinical level, they were significantly interfering with his life. Mark was almost anxious, a very real problem that needed correcting. In addition to the distress he felt, being almost anxious put his physical health at risk. Researchers have found that anxiety symptoms point to an increased risk for certain diseases (like coronary heart disease) and overall mortality.[1] Furthermore, if he hadn't sought help, his anxiety may have continued to worsen until it reached a severe level. Indeed, many people who are almost anxious might never seek help for their worries—

because they might not even realize they have a problem that can be solved.

I am writing this book for the vast number of readers like Mark, who don't quite fit a diagnostic "label" of anxiety and too often do not seek or receive the help they need. If you have spent a great amount of your life being plagued by "a little too much" anxiety, this book will give you the tools to finally find relief.

Bringing your anxiety down to a healthier level can help you find more enjoyment in your days, experience a better family and work environment, and eliminate the emotional, mental, and even physical problems that anxiety can cause, such as muscle tension, gastrointestinal distress, and a racing heart.

Tackling almost anxiety requires seeing anxiety in a new way. In this book, you will learn a new way of thinking about anxiety and a new set of skills to help you maintain your anxiety at a level that is "just right" (not too little and not too much).

I hope that when you're finished reading, you'll be using your anxiety as a motor to propel yourself through life, with the ability to approach anxiety-provoking situations instead of avoiding them.

◆

Part 1

Anxiety:
Too Much, Too Little, Just Right

1

What Is "Almost Anxious"?

On a blazing afternoon in July 2003, I learned a lesson on how to keep a healthy perspective on anxiety.

Hiking had never been my strong suit, especially hiking at high altitudes. Yet here I was near the end of the Half Dome trail in California's Yosemite National Park. I was drawn to Yosemite, and to this trail in particular, because of my love for Ansel Adams's photos of the area. Yosemite Valley has been described as "not just a great valley, but a shrine to human foresight, the strength of granite, the power of glaciers, the persistence of life, and the tranquility of the High Sierra."[1] After such a powerful description, how could I not want to hike its Half Dome trail . . . even if it's a treacherous 8.5-mile climb up a 5,000-foot peak?

I had been hiking uphill since 4 a.m. For most of the hike, I'd been covered by a canopy of beautiful forest. The landscape suddenly shifted as I approached the base of Half Dome. In front of me stood a bald granite face that seemed to go straight up and disappear into the sky. Ascending the last 400 feet to the top would require gripping two steel cables and holding on (for dear life!) as I walked up with emptiness on either side of me.

My heart pounded, my sweating increased, my body tensed, and I slowed my pace. All I could think about was "What if I slip and fall?" The more I focused on that thought, the more my body reacted. I began scanning my surroundings for rocks with edges that I could grab in case I stumbled. My sense of apprehension increased. My friend who was hiking with me asked if I was okay. I answered, "I'm not sure; I might have a height phobia." He raised his eyebrows and remarked, "And you choose *now* to tell me?"

Maggie's Story

Several years later, a young woman named Maggie sat in my office. Maggie was nineteen years old, originally from South America (like me), and studying abroad in the United States for the first time. You might not have known that Maggie was from another country had she not told you, since her spoken English was impeccable and she immediately engaged in a detailed discussion of the upcoming presidential election. Maggie experienced her first-ever panic attack while walking to class during her freshman year of college.

The attack came out of the blue, and she could not pinpoint anything that led to it: "I was walking to class when suddenly I noticed my heart starting to pound. I began to feel nauseated and had difficulty breathing. My mind started to race and I had trouble focusing. I started getting sweaty and it felt like someone was sitting on my chest. I believed I was having a heart attack. I nearly went to the emergency room, but, thankfully,

I was able to reach my mom on the phone. She distracted me from my anxiety and helped me calm down enough that I was able to go to class."

Despite this scary experience, Maggie described herself as happy, with many friends, and very lucky to have gotten a scholarship to study in the United States. At our first meeting, she was only mildly worried about the attack, but she had sought help at the request of her mother, who had battled panic disorder for most of her life.

Does Maggie have full-fledged panic disorder? Do I have a diagnosable phobia of heights? Alternatively, perhaps we are both feeling the normal physical sensations that are designed to help protect us in threatening situations. Or are we somewhere in the "almost anxious" space in between? To answer that question, it is helpful to know a little more about anxiety and its evolutionary benefits.

Why Humans Have Anxiety: A Brief History

Imagine if Maggie had lived thousands of years ago and instead of walking across campus to go to class she was walking through a dense jungle. Walking through a jungle thousands (and even hundreds) of years ago, our ancestors had to be alert, focused, watchful, and ready to attack an animal for dinner or fight off an enemy to stay alive—as do tribal peoples who still hunt for their food today. If Maggie stumbled across a lion during her walk, her body's first response would be to go into a fight-or-flight mode.

- Her heart would speed up, as she would need more blood moving through her body to get her muscles ready to fight the lion or flee from it. A stronger heartbeat also leads to more blood circulation, which in turn would raise Maggie's body temperature.

- She would get sweaty, which has two primary functions: to decrease her body temperature (this is important to keep her brain cool!) and to make her body more slippery, which would make it harder for an attacker to grab her.

- Her muscle tension would increase. With a little luck, her tightly wound muscles would propel her safely out of the lion's grasp.

- If Maggie had just eaten prior to seeing the lion, she likely would start to feel nauseated and she might have stomach cramps. In an extreme circumstance, she might even feel the pangs of diarrhea, since her body would stop digesting food to ensure instead that blood was available to her muscles to help her run.

Do these symptoms sound familiar? They did to Maggie. All of these sensations are identical to what she experienced during her panic attack late that fall. They were also the same sensations I felt when looking up to the top of Half Dome. This is our bodies' alarm system and it looks similar regardless of what triggers the alarm.

If Maggie had been facing a lion in the jungle when she had those sensations, she would have really appreciated what her body was doing. A jolt of the hormone adrenaline—or the burst of anxiety that results from it—is essential to survival when humans run into lions in the jungle. People facing immediate danger need these jolts to survive.

Physical sensations like these are uncomfortable and even scary when you're having them, especially when they come out of the blue, but they are not the enemy. Just the opposite: the fight-or-flight response is what kept humans alive through history.

As you start looking at your anxiety in new ways, this is the first lesson I'd like you to keep in mind: these symptoms are simply tools that evolution has hardwired into our bodies to help us survive. This will give you a starting point for changing the way you think about anxiety-related sensations so they're not so startling.

From Fight-or-Flight Response to a False Alarm

You can think about the fight-or-flight response as an alarm system set to go off when you are in danger. As helpful as this system is, there are two ways in which the alarm system can cause you some trouble. The first is when there is a false alarm.

Maggie's experience of having a panic attack is not unusual. People can experience panic attacks even without having a full-blown panic disorder—a common form of anxiety disorder characterized by recurrent panic attacks. In fact, the results of a national survey suggest that 28 percent of people will experience a panic attack at some point in their lives, but only 4.7 percent of people meet the diagnostic criteria for panic disorder in their lifetimes.[2] So why do some people develop panic disorder, while millions of others don't?

One reason people develop panic disorder is their misinterpretation of the consequences associated with their physical sensations. It's easier to understand this with an example.

Imagine that you are at the mall, shopping for shoes, when you notice that everyone in the store is running quickly toward the door.

What is the first thought that comes to mind? Fire!

What do you feel? Most people would start to feel the fight-or-flight impulse. The heart pumps faster. Muscles tense.

What would you do? I know I would run if I thought the store were on fire, likely fast and without questioning it. How about you?

But, suppose that before dropping your shoes and running for the door, you were to stop another shopper and ask, "Hey, what is going on?" And the shopper told you that Brad Pitt had just been seen elsewhere in the mall shooting a movie! How would this piece of information change your natural fight-or-flight response? True fans might still run. Yet they would now be running with a smile and the hope of seeing the movie star. For others, like myself, our bodies might relax and we might just keep browsing for shoes. (I have to confess, if it were the exciting Colombian entertainer Shakira, I might run to see *her*!)

Your body is wired to respond in a particular way when your alarm goes off. But, as you see, at times that response is not appropriate. Sometimes there is no real danger. Sometimes the body is responding to a false alarm. This is what happened to Maggie. As she was walking to class, she noticed her heart was beating a little faster than usual. Perhaps she was concerned about her class or perhaps she was simply walking fast enough to get her heart pumping a little harder than usual. Whatever the reason, when she noticed her heart beating quickly, her brain misinterpreted those physical sensations as something dangerous, yelled "Fire!" and kicked her alarm system into full gear. But, as she would later realize, there was no danger. It was a false alarm.

Live a Better Life with the Yerkes-Dodson Curve

Although false alarms occasionally occur, much of the time our alarm system works as it is supposed to, going off when there is something important that we need to pay attention to. Fortunately for us, fighting lions isn't the only time some anxiety can be helpful. In today's world, you're likely to encounter situations that drop your body into this emergency mode over and over through the course of a day: the radio doesn't go off on time when you need to wake up, the computer crashes during an important project, or your spouse starts an argument when you are already overwhelmed.

In short, higher anxiety, when it's linked to specific situations and doesn't expand to fill up too much of your attention, can be helpful. This anxiety allows a mother to jump and catch her baby daughter before she falls from a chair or a student to concentrate harder while taking an important exam. It helped me hold on tight to those cables as I climbed to the top of the mountain. But when does normal anxiety cross the line and become almost anxiety? As two Harvard scientists found, the line that defines the healthy level of anxiety is actually pretty easy to find.

In 1908, Robert M. Yerkes and John D. Dodson conducted a series of experiments with mice to learn about the relationship between electric shock intensity and performance.[3] They found that performance on difficult tasks increased with increasing shock intensity up to a point and then began to decrease. These experiments suggested that an increase in physiological arousal (in other words, alertness) is directly associated with an increase in one's ability to perform a task—but only up to a point. Psychologists now call this the "Yerkes-Dodson Law."

This is easy to understand if you think about that first cup of coffee in the morning, which raises your body's level of arousal and helps you focus a little better. (No wonder Starbucks has lines out the door every morning!)

But drinking more and more coffee doesn't send your performance levels continuously higher in a straight line. Eventually, the coffee produces an unwanted effect. If you have too many cups of coffee, you feel jitters, a pounding heart, less ability to focus, and an overall *decrease* in productivity.

Similarly, the Yerkes-Dodson Law suggests that the increase in performance related to the increase in arousal—a word that we can also take to mean "anxiety"—only goes so far. As figure 3 illustrates, moderate levels of arousal are associated with an increase in mental and physical performance. Yerkes and Dodson showed that the level of anxiety that fuels optimal performance lies about midway through the curve.

For decades, mental health professionals have called this "adaptive anxiety." This is like being in "the zone," which often leads to increased focus, creativity, problem solving, and multitasking. Often athletes will describe such feelings while they're competing, with the sense that their minds are quiet and focused. Most people have had similar experiences; at times, they feel as though their minds are without distraction and they are able to fully focus on the task at hand, productive and happy. I often find myself in the zone immediately after a "hot yoga" class (in fact, most of this book was written during these periods!).

At these moments, you have some anxiety fueling your good feelings—you just aren't very aware of it.

Figure 3.

Adaptation of Yerkes-Dodson Curve to Almost Anxious

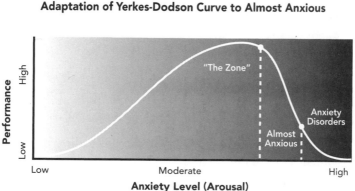

The Yerkes-Dodson curve teaches us that "the zone" is the state in which anxiety and arousal are moderate but performance is high, when you are using anxiety to propel your life forward.

The curve also makes clear what happens when people become *too* anxious. After a point, greater anxiety causes your performance to suffer. You may not work as quickly. You may have trouble focusing your attention. Your once-motivating thoughts turn to fears and worries, distracting you from your task at hand. Unpleasant physical sensations, like Maggie's pounding heartbeat, take you further away from a normal, fully productive life.

This is the second way in which our alarm system can cause us some trouble: when the alarm is a little too loud and the anxiety becomes just a bit too much. As the graph reveals, this is when you become almost anxious and your performance starts to decrease. Indeed, research has shown that people with mild to moderate anxiety (as compared with individuals with normal anxiety) report increased functional impairment, which includes reduced ability to work, get along with others, and take care of themselves.[4]

"The Zone" versus "Almost Anxious"

I define "almost anxious" as the problem that arises when you spend most of your time somewhere to the right of "the zone" and the left of "anxiety disorder" on the Yerkes-Dodson curve. In other words, this is the state when anxiety begins to interfere with your life but isn't severe enough to warrant a diagnosis of an anxiety disorder.

How Can You Know Whether Your Anxiety Is Helpful or Unhelpful?

If a car is speeding toward you while you're crossing the street, you want that burst of anxiety that prompts you to leap out of the way. When you have a big project due at work, you want a proper amount of anxiety to motivate you to complete it on time. In these examples, my patients can easily understand why adaptive anxiety—the term mental health professionals use for "healthy" anxiety—can be useful.

But my patients often respond, "But no car is coming toward me in the middle of the night when I am lying awake in bed with my mind racing and my heart pounding!" And they are right. Anxiety is no longer helpful when

- it doesn't shut off when you're out of danger.
- it flares up at inappropriate times.
- it keeps you from living your life.

Instead, it's a problem that needs solving.

How Can You Know Whether You Have Almost Anxiety or a Full-Blown, Diagnosable Anxiety Disorder?

In the next chapter, I'll discuss the difference between almost anxiety and anxiety disorders in more depth. To get started answering this question, you can complete the easy screening questionnaire known as the GAD-7. (The questionnaire is presented in exercise 1, or you can download it at www.Almost Anxious.com.)

This seven-question scale is well supported as a reliable and valid measure of common anxiety symptoms. In other words, the GAD-7 does a good job of identifying people who may have an anxiety disorder, whether a generalized anxiety disorder (GAD), social anxiety disorder, or panic disorder. Higher scores on the GAD-7 indicate more severe anxiety symptoms.[5] Even though it's quite short, the GAD-7 has been shown to perform as well as longer anxiety questionnaires.[6]

Exercise 1.
GAD-7 Questionnaire

During the last two weeks, how often have you been
bothered by the following problems? Rate each of the statements
in the table below using a scale of 0 to 3, with 0 meaning
"not at all" and 3 meaning "nearly every day."

Not at all	Several days	More than half the days	Nearly every day	
0	1	2	3	My Score
1.	Feeling nervous, anxious, or on edge			
2.	Not being able to stop or control worrying			
3.	Worrying too much about different things			
4.	Trouble relaxing			
5.	Being so restless that it is hard to sit still			
6.	Becoming easily annoyed or irritable			
7.	Feeling afraid, as if something awful might happen			
Total score (sum of all scores)				

What was your number? Here's what the results of one
study suggest:

- A score of 0 to 4 points represents minimal anxiety.

- A score of 5 to 9 represents mild anxiety.

- A score of 10 or higher represents moderate to
  severe anxiety that likely meets diagnostic criteria
  for a clinical disorder.[7]

For our purposes, a score of 5 to 9 points means that you
probably fall into the almost anxious category. However, this
range should not be considered a hard-and-fast rule. If your

score is hovering around an 8 or 9, you may indeed have an anxiety disorder.

Figure 4.
Anxiety Scale Showing GAD-7 Ranges

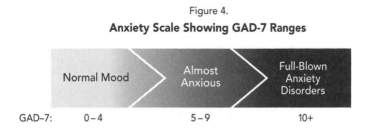

| GAD–7: | 0 – 4 | 5 – 9 | 10+ |

If using the tools in this book isn't enough to bring your anxiety down to a comfortable level, you may want to consider seeking professional treatment (see chapter 12). If your score on this questionnaire is 10 or higher, you may have a full-fledged anxiety disorder. In this case, consult with a mental health care provider for assistance.

How Common Is Almost Anxiety?

Research suggests that approximately 24 percent of the general population scores between 5 and 9 on the GAD-7.[8] In other words, nearly one out of four people is almost anxious. What these numbers should tell you is that being almost anxious is very common. At one point or another, most people will experience some of the symptoms described in this book. So, if you scored between a 5 and 9 on the GAD-7, you're in good company!

Why Is It Important to Tackle My Almost Anxiety?

You may have mixed feelings about reducing your anxiety. There have likely been times when your anxiety was helpful. It may have pushed you to work harder on an important project or study more for a test. If so, you may feel like you're not quite ready to give up your anxiety. When considering whether to tackle your almost anxiety, there are two important things to consider. First, almost anxiety can be harmful to your physical and mental health. Experts refer to almost anxiety as a "subthreshold" condition, meaning the symptoms fall below the level required for a diagnosis of an anxiety disorder. Nonetheless, many studies suggest that subthreshold anxiety-related conditions are associated with significant life interference. For example, people with subthreshold panic disorder are at increased risk for other psychiatric disorders, including depression and substance use problems.[9] Individuals with subthreshold social anxiety are also at increased risk for other psychiatric disorders, and they report lower life satisfaction and greater work disability.[10] Second, addressing almost anxiety does not mean you will never experience anxiety again. The goal of this book is to teach you how to bring your anxiety from a level that is negatively affecting your life back to the zone where you are actually benefiting from the sense of moderately heightened arousal that evolution gave to you.

Maggie's Outcome

Maggie is a great example of someone who is almost anxious. Even though she had some mild anxiety and distress associated with the panic attacks, she was still engaging in her day-to-day life and was not significantly impaired by this distress. Yet she was engaging in some *avoidance behaviors*. Much like an ostrich that sticks its head in the sand when it is afraid, humans may try to avoid things that make them anxious. Maggie avoided drinking coffee or exercising because it brought on physical sensations that she associated with her panic attacks. When people avoid anxiety-provoking situations, they come to believe that those situations are more and more dangerous.[11] As a result, some individuals with almost anxiety go on to develop a full-blown anxiety disorder.

To help Maggie learn that these sensations are not dangerous, we had her confront them. At first, she was skeptical that her panic-like sensations would not harm her (after all, they felt horrible!). As time went on, however, she started to learn that her sensations were merely a false alarm and not an actual dangerous situation. In one session, we had a shot of espresso and I asked her to spin around in my office chair as fast as she could (sometimes my patients find that counseling sessions can be an adventure!). This was the perfect way to bring on the heart-pounding sensations and dizziness that Maggie experienced during her panic attack.

These techniques are supported by research studies and are called "interoceptive exposure."[12] Specifically, researchers have shown that the way to treat panic-like sensations is to actually induce the very symptoms that the person fears. In Maggie's case, I asked her to drink espresso to get her heart pounding, which forced her to face a sensation she would normally avoid. I also encouraged her to "ride her wave of anxiety" (that is, stay on top of it, rather than feel crushed by it), and experience the heart pounding as the false alarm it truly was, which in turn naturally decreased her symptoms.

I encouraged her to experience these sensations but not to try to change them. She learned to stand her ground and observe the sensations rather than try to confront them or run from them.

During our sessions, I also had her examine how she interpreted the consequences of her panic attack. At first, Maggie was certain that another panic attack could cause her to go crazy or lose control of her actions. However, by having panic-like sensations in my office without reacting to them, she was able to experience firsthand that her "false alarm" didn't have to lead anywhere harmful.

In short, by breaking the connection between her physical sensations and her subsequent thoughts about them, Maggie learned not to be afraid of the feelings associated with anxiety or panic. She was able to return to activities in her life that she would have previously avoided, like her morning coffee and distance runs. By the end of our work together, Maggie would joke that even though she still felt like something within her was trying to get her anxiety elevated, she no longer felt the need to respond to it, because it was merely a fire drill—not an actual fire that needed attention.

• • •

Anxiety disorders are very common in our society and all over the world, so odds are good that you know someone who has had a full-blown anxiety disorder. Being almost anxious is a different problem, though it has much in common with anxiety disorders. In the next chapter, I'll show you how to tell the difference between them and explain why understanding this difference is so important.

❖

2

The Many "Flavors" of Anxiety

In the introduction, I talked about Mark, whose mounting worry was interfering with both his sleep and his relationship with his girlfriend.

After meeting with Mark, I concluded that he didn't have a true anxiety disorder. Instead, he was struggling with *almost* anxiety, which I worked with him to relieve. In the previous chapter, you learned whether your own anxiety is at the healthy level that keeps you in "the zone" and propels your life forward or whether you have instead moved into almost anxiety.

In this chapter, I'd like to discuss the difference between being almost anxious and having its more serious relatives, the anxiety disorders. Given that disorders occur along a spectrum, and there can be a slippery slope from almost anxious to a full-blown anxiety disorder, it is important for you to know the indicators of a full disorder in case you are moving that way.

For this discussion, let's meet Ricardo, who shares some characteristics with Mark yet meets the criteria for a more serious problem.

Ricardo's Story

I treated Ricardo for generalized anxiety disorder, which is a full-fledged type of anxiety disorder. Like Mark, Ricardo was in his mid-thirties, single, and well educated. "Doc, I've always been a worrier," he said, again echoing what Mark told me.

"My parents used to make fun of me when I was younger, because I worried about everything. I worried if they were not home on time; I worried about my homework; I worried if my parents would be able to pay their bills; I worried whether I was going to make friends in school. In fact, *I don't remember a day in my life when I didn't worry most of the day.* I don't even know how I finished college with all of my worrying!" he said.

Ricardo's worries had created lots of problems for him. For starters, he had a very short temper, often feeling on edge and irritable. Coming from a Latino culture where it was okay to express strong emotions, Ricardo was not concerned about his temper. "Men cry at the soccer stadium, hug each other, and yell," he rationalized.

Yet Ricardo failed to notice that his irritability was not limited to socially acceptable displays of emotion. He told me that he could not date women for more than a few months, because he would lose his temper and yell when he was irritated, which in turn caused them to flee the relationship. "But if they can't take my level of passion, why would they go for a Latin man?" he wondered.

Because Ricardo was always on edge, he often felt exhausted

by the end of the day and suffered from muscle tension. With his level of anxiety, I was not surprised to hear that Ricardo was having trouble falling asleep—he would lie in bed for hours worrying about what the worry was doing to his life.

When I learned about the depth of Ricardo's worry and irritability, I was able to determine that he was well beyond being almost anxious. Instead, he was feeling the impact of generalized anxiety disorder.

What a Full-blown Anxiety Disorder Looks Like

To diagnose an emotional, mood, or personality disorder (problems that affect your brain chemistry), mental health professionals must learn whether the person's difficulties meet the criteria in the *Diagnostic and Statistical Manual of Mental Disorders (DSM)*. The *DSM* has gone through multiple revisions; in 2013 the profession transitioned from using the *DSM-IV-TR* (commonly called the *DSM-4*) to the *DSM-5* (see the appendix).[1]

To be diagnosed with generalized anxiety disorder, a person must have significant levels of worry more days than not for at least six months, in addition to at least two other symptoms from a list of concerns, such as difficulty concentrating, sleep problems, irritability, and muscle tension.

The main difference between Mark's and Ricardo's experience with anxiety centered on the persistence of their worry. Although both men said they'd always been worriers, Ricardo had been bothered by his worries more days than not. Mark, by contrast, had been experiencing a lot of worry since his promotion, but it had not been so severe and intense for the majority of his life, or even for more than the past three months.

The severity of their worry also separated the two men. Whereas Mark's worries were interfering with his sleep and ability to concentrate at work, Ricardo was plagued with constant worry that was bothersome enough to impede nearly all areas of his life. In addition to the sleep and focus troubles that Mark faced, Ricardo's anxiety was translating into problems with his social life, work life, and even physical health.

Another important factor that separates an anxiety disorder from normal anxiety and almost anxiety is whether symptoms have a *contextual relationship* to your life experiences. Is your anxiety appropriate for the situation? If you have been put on probation at work and your boss warned that you might lose your job, you might have a good reason to worry. If, like Mark, you're in good standing at work, your anxiety might be disproportionate to the situation but still not persistent and severe enough to be an anxiety disorder.

When I think about Ricardo, who worried as a child about his parents paying the bills, despite no indication that they were having financial struggles, it is hard to consider his worries appropriate to the situation. As such, Ricardo's worries were not only persistent and excessive in general; they were also excessive to his particular situation.

Ricardo also noticed that, much like the children's game of Whac-A-Mole, whenever he was able to solve one problem in his life, a new problem immediately popped up. Through therapy, he realized that the real issue wasn't having each of these everyday problems; it was his constant state of worry.

In sum, although Mark and Ricardo both had significant levels of anxiety, only Ricardo would be diagnosed with an anxiety disorder if he were evaluated by a trained mental health professional.

Four Anxiety Disorders That Have *Almost* Versions

Not all anxiety is created alike. Experts group anxiety disorders into different categories with different names. To be diagnosed with one of these problems, a person has to have a specific set of symptoms that cause significant interference or distress.

The way that mental health professionals define anxiety has been shifting. The diagnostic criteria outlined in the *DSM-5* differ significantly from what was in the *DSM-IV-TR*. Among the most notable changes is that post-traumatic stress disorder (PTSD) and obsessive-compulsive disorder (OCD) are no longer placed under the umbrella of anxiety disorders. Although experts still believe that PTSD and OCD are similar to anxiety disorders, they are now considered sufficiently different to warrant separating them into their own categories. For example, new research suggests that different brain circuitry is involved in OCD compared with the other anxiety disorders.[2] As such, I won't be discussing these problems in depth in this book.

Among the remaining anxiety disorders, these four are the most often studied and most common:

- generalized anxiety disorder
- panic disorder, with and without agoraphobia
- social anxiety disorder
- specific phobias, such as those involving heights or animals

Anxiety Worldwide

Rates of generalized anxiety disorder differ across regions and cultures, and they're typically lower in non-Western nations. Although the reason for this difference is unclear, one explanation may be that worry may be less likely to meet the "excessiveness" criterion for people living in a developing nation and dealing with extreme economic or other stress.

Panic disorder is far less common in non-Western and less-developed countries, with fewer than 1 percent having it during their lives in nations such as Mexico, Nigeria, Japan, and South Africa. As with GAD, the reason for this difference in prevalence rates is unclear. It may be that psychiatric assessment tools that were developed in Western countries do not adequately capture cultural differences in the expression of anxiety.[3]

Although many anxiety disorders seem to be more common in Western countries, anxiety is nonetheless a disruptive disorder regardless of boundaries and borders. According to a study conducted by the World Health Organization's World Mental Health Survey Initiative, anxiety disorders were the most common type of psychiatric disorder in ten of seventeen countries surveyed, having affected 4.8 to 31 percent of people in countries around the globe at some point during their lives.[4]

However, anxiety symptoms present somewhat differently across cultures. For instance, *ataque de nervios* (literally translated to "attack of nerves") is a panic-like condition most prevalent in Latino cultures. It is characterized by many of the same physical symptoms of panic attacks (feeling faint, fear of "going crazy"), but unlike a panic attack that comes out of nowhere, this often occurs as a direct result of a distressing situation. Moreover, an *ataque de nervios* marked by extreme displays of emotion is often viewed as a culturally appropriate means of expressing despair.

Another culturally specific example is *trúng gió* ("being hit by the wind"), a common symptom in Vietnamese refugees, much like the chills and dizziness experienced in panic, but explained as the effect of a harmful wind on the body. Similarly, in Cambodia, panic-like symptoms such as nausea, dizziness, and heart pounding are explained as a sudden surge of *khyal*, or "wind attack."

The prevalence of different phobias also varies around the world. For example, children and adolescents in Australia and the United States more often report phobias of getting lost and being robbed, whereas children and adolescents in China and Nigeria more often report fears of animals and getting shocked by electricity.[5] Additionally, individuals in Western countries are more likely to report feeling detached from reality or detached from their bodies during panic attacks.[6] Thus, although anxiety occurs worldwide, there are cultural differences in its expression, such as the object of fear, and the emphasis on specific symptoms.[7]

As with the symptoms of anxiety disorders, it is likely that the symptoms of being almost anxious vary across cultures.

Here's a primer on these disorders so you can better understand their *almost* versions:

Generalized Anxiety Disorder

Generalized anxiety disorder (GAD) brings chronic, persistent, and intense worry and anxiety that extends across many areas of one's life. Although estimates vary, a recent study reported that 2 percent of adults and adolescents in the United States have GAD each year, and about 4.3 percent have had GAD at some point during their lives.[8]

For people with GAD, constant worry tends to run their lives. Many individuals with GAD also report that anxiety gets in the way of their decision making or causes them to avoid situations, leading to negative consequences. Additionally, people diagnosed with GAD often spend a great deal of time preparing for these situations, and they often require reassurance from others to help soothe their worries.

Ming-Cho's Story

Ming-Cho, a seventy-four-year-old widow whom I treated, described her GAD as the "war of her mind." She said she felt like her mind was always running quickly, with her thoughts competing with each other for her attention. When she was younger and still working as a newspaper editor, Ming-Cho would spend hours trying to focus at work, without much success. Her symptoms of GAD were so severe that it would take her twice as long as her colleagues to get her job done. As a result, she would always leave work late and exhausted. Ming-Cho would be the first to say, "I am a worrywart. I worry about worrying."

Not only did Ming-Cho bear the burden of an overactive mind, she also had a lot of physical symptoms related to her worry. Her body was always tense. She could not sit still, often pacing in her office instead of editing the daily columns of her newspaper. While pacing, Ming-Cho would fret about dinner, her kids, her grandchildren, and upcoming social events. Her worries were present all the time for most of her life, which is why her symptoms would be severe enough to conclude that she had GAD.

Panic Disorder

As we discussed earlier, panic disorder (PD) is an anxiety disorder marked by recurrent, unexpected panic attacks that are sudden and lead to extreme discomfort and uneasiness. About 2 percent of adults and adolescents in the United States have had panic disorder in the past year, and about 4 percent have had it in their lifetime.[9]

To be diagnosed with panic disorder, a person must have at least one panic attack that is completely out of the blue. People with other anxiety disorders, like GAD, might also experience panic attacks, but usually these attacks are triggered by something identifiable such as worries, social fears, or anticipatory anxiety related to future events (for example, a work presentation).

In addition to having an out-of-the-blue panic attack, to be diagnosed with panic disorder, a person also has to be concerned about having an additional panic attack or substantially change his or her behavior to avoid having another panic attack. Often people will worry about "going crazy," "dying," or "not being able to escape or get help" while having a panic attack.

To find out if you have experienced panic attacks, work through the checklist in exercise 2. You can also download this exercise at www.AlmostAnxious.com.

Exercise 2.
Panic Attack Checklist:
Does a Panic Attack Mean I'm More Than Almost Anxious?

A panic attack—sometimes called an anxiety attack—is defined as an intense surge of anxiety and fear, with a very fast onset, combined with *at least four* of the following symptoms. To determine whether you have indeed had a panic attack, think back to the last time you had a lot of panic and anxiety and check the following boxes if the symptoms happened at the same time and bothered you significantly.

- ☐ sweating
- ☐ fear of dying
- ☐ trembling or shaking
- ☐ choking feeling
- ☐ chest pain or discomfort
- ☐ nausea or abdominal distress
- ☐ chills or warm sensations
- ☐ numbness or tingling sensations
- ☐ fear of losing control or "going crazy"
- ☐ shortness of breath or smothering sensation
- ☐ feeling dizzy, unsteady, lightheaded, or faint
- ☐ feelings of unreality, like things are happening in slow motion or not in real time
- ☐ feeling detached from your body, as if you were having an "out-of-body experience"
- ☐ palpitations, pounding heart, or accelerated heart rate

If you have ever experienced a panic attack, it doesn't mean that you have a full-fledged anxiety disorder, such as panic disorder, or even that you are almost anxious. Studies show that the experience of panic itself is not uncommon and that people's response to their panic attacks can lead to more problems.

For example, if you begin avoiding things as a result of your panic attack, you are more likely over time to develop what mental health professionals consider a panic disorder. In contrast, if you dismiss the attack as a one-time experience and do not let it keep affecting you, you might never have another one.

The most extreme cases of panic disorder might also be accompanied by agoraphobia. This term comes from the Greek word *agora* (meaning "marketplace"), and it represents the fear of not being able to escape public situations while having panic attacks, which in turn can cause a person to become home-bound. Although agoraphobia can also occur in the absence of panic disorder, the fear usually still revolves around not being able to escape public situations if one has panic-like symptoms or becomes incapacitated. Approximately 2 percent of adults and adolescents in the United States have had agoraphobia (with or without panic disorder) in the past year, and 2.5 percent have had agoraphobia (with or without panic disorder) at some point in their lives.[10]

George's Story

George, a man I had a phone consultation with, had been housebound for five years after experiencing a severe panic attack while driving to work. George was taken to the emergency room, convinced he was having a soon-to-be-fatal heart attack. The entire ordeal was so upsetting that he took some time off work to try to get better. Unfortunately, every time he tried to leave his house, he would start to panic and become scared that he might not be able to get help.

He started to order anything he needed online, thus further reinforcing his avoidance of social situations. When his sick leave ran out, George still found it impossible to return to work, and he ended up losing his job. During our phone call, I strongly urged George to seek help for his agoraphobia, but the thought of leaving the house was so scary to him that he was too paralyzed to do so. His story demonstrates how *avoiding* the things that trigger your anxiety helps reinforce the disorder.

Social Anxiety Disorder

Social anxiety disorder (SAD) is one of the most common mental disorders. Approximately 7 percent of adults and adolescents in the United States are affected by SAD each year, and about 11 percent have had SAD at some point in their lives.[11] Individuals with SAD have persistently heightened fear or anxiety in response to social situations, especially situations that cause them to face scrutiny or judgment from other people.

People with SAD often report fear that's linked to performance anxiety, for example, from giving a talk or a presentation at work. SAD is also characterized by fear of social interactions (such as meeting someone for the first time) or situations in which the person could be observed (such as eating in public).

Although most people might feel uneasy in *some* social situations, like going on a blind date or speaking in front of 500 people, with social anxiety disorder, the fear of being observed and judged by others, or of humiliating or embarrassing oneself, is distorted by anxiety. Often, people with SAD misinterpret ambiguous social cues (such as an audience member not making eye contact during a presentation) as a sign that they did something wrong.

One marked difference between someone with normal

social fears and someone with SAD involves the degree of impairment related to the disorder. Although most people might not enjoy public speaking, when their job is on the line, they face it and try to do their best. People with social anxiety disorder, however, will avoid the situation. In other words, they'll get out of the talk even if it hurts their standing at work. In fact, most of the people with SAD who I've treated have changed career paths or limited their educational choices to minimize their exposure to social situations where they might be the focus of attention. This avoidance is probably why SAD often leads to negative outcomes, such as poorer work performance, higher unemployment rates, and impaired social life.[12]

My patient Dwayne was a good example of someone whose education and romantic life was stifled under the weight of social anxiety disorder.

Dwayne's Story

Dwayne was an attractive forty-three-year-old African American carpenter. When I first met Dwayne, he would not make eye contact with me. He was very shy and spoke in a soft manner, watching his words carefully and seeking my reassurance that he had not offended me with his comments. Dwayne had been a shy kid with very few friends in grade school and middle school. Still, he managed to get good grades. It was not until Dwayne moved to a new city during high school that his social fears became debilitating.

Dwayne's mother moved him and his four siblings from the Bronx in New York to an affluent suburb to ensure a better education for her kids after Dwayne's father died of a heart attack at age forty-two. Dwayne had tears in his eyes as he described his first day of high school: "That is when my life became hell. All of the kids were different from me. They dressed differently, talked differently, and I could not fit in." Dwayne noted that he felt embarrassed and humiliated by the other kids, all of whom were white. In retrospect, he realized that most of what happened was only in his head, since the classmates weren't actually doing anything to make him feel bad.

As a result of his fears, Dwayne avoided his classmates, and by the end of his freshman year, he started wanting to skip school. Dwayne would get so anxious before class presentations that he would have panic-like symptoms, which were sometimes so intense that he would have a full-blown panic attack. Although he somehow managed to finish school, his fears and anxiety exacted a high price during these years: he was not able to date, socialize, or make many friends.

As an adult, Dwayne found his carpentry work fulfilling, but he never got married or had kids. In his own words: "I think I would die before I approached a girl."

Specific Phobias

Phobias are another common type of psychiatric disorder that in the United States affect about 12 percent of adults and adolescents each year and about 16 percent of adults and adolescents during their lifetime.[13]

Some common phobias involve

- heights.
- certain creatures such as snakes or insects.
- blood and injections.
- closed-in spaces.
- flying.

Similar to social phobia, with these phobias the feared object or situation is associated with persistent anxiety and fear, and is often avoided at all costs. To receive a diagnosis of a specific phobia, the active avoidance and fear of the object in question must be significant enough to interfere with one's life.[14] Consider my experience facing the long, frightening ascent to the top of Half Dome. Although it is likely that I have some of the symptoms of a height phobia, which surfaced on that hiking trip at Yosemite National Park, I wouldn't meet the criteria for a diagnosis since I don't completely avoid heights. (To test this idea, I actually went skydiving—twice!)

Ricardo's Outcome

Ricardo came to me with uncontrollable worries that kept his mind racing. These led to a host of physical and emotional consequences, such as sleep disturbance, muscle tension, difficulty concentrating, fatigue, irritability, and edginess. I worked with him for twenty sessions to help him reduce symptoms of generalized anxiety disorder to a more constructive level of anxiety.

In other words, Ricardo used therapy to get back into "the zone," which is also the objective when you're almost anxious.

Our first goal in treatment was to help Ricardo learn how his brain was working and why his thoughts got stuck in the "anxious wheel" of *thinking* about his anxious thoughts (I'll talk more about this in chapter 5). After a few sessions, Ricardo started to notice that whenever he had a scary thought, he assumed that it was completely true and fact based. But upon further examination, he discovered that his assumptions were rarely based on evidence.

For example, he once became terrified that he was going to be fired during his annual review. The more he thought about the upcoming review, the more anxious he became. As we worked together to slow down his brain so he could evaluate his thoughts, Ricardo was able to think of a list of facts that contradicted his original thoughts—including that he had increased his company's overall revenue by 5 percent in one business deal that year, which he knew made a good impression on his boss.

Ricardo discovered that he avoided his fears (in this case, his own worries) by focusing on other less distressing worries. For example, for his review with his boss, he had to make a list of how he met his yearly goals, but instead of doing that, which made him worried that he would be fired, he would focus on other less important tasks, like answering his email.

Although the momentary attention shift would decrease Ricardo's anxiety in the short term, as soon as his thoughts returned to the annual review, he would start to worry again. To counter this, Ricardo resolved to practice working on his yearly goals and accomplishments for the first thirty minutes of each day for a week, thus facing his worries instead of avoiding them.

Over time, Ricardo worked his way down to being just almost anxious, and then he reduced his anxiety further to reach a healthy level. By the end of our work together, Ricardo commented that he knew he might still have moments of high worry in his life, but with the skills he developed in our work together, he felt well equipped to fight the GAD if it ever came back in full force.

• • •

Ricardo's story is just one example of how cognitive-behavioral therapy (CBT), a psychological treatment method that targets problematic thoughts and behaviors, helps patients deal with anxiety. Indeed, the results of numerous studies show that CBT is an effective treatment for full-fledged anxiety disorders.[15] It is likely that CBT works for almost anxiety too.

In part 3 of this book, I'll provide tips on using the principles of anxiety-reducing CBT in your own life. But first, I'd like to discuss some other emotional or physical problems that can occur alongside anxiety. If you have these issues, such as depression or substance use, they're likely to interfere with your efforts to manage your anxiety.

■ ◆ ■

3

Am I Almost Anxious...
and Something Else?

If you are having symptoms that fit with what we're describing as almost anxiety, you will probably notice that these symptoms rarely show up alone. Think back over your life: Was there a time when you felt anxious without any other disruptions? Or do your anxiety symptoms come with physical complaints like headaches or upset stomach?

The mind and body are closely entwined. When one becomes out of balance, the other often follows. That's why when you're trying to uncover the source of your almost anxious symptoms, it's important to consider whether some other psychological problem—or possibly a physical concern—is actually the cause.

When trying to untangle two problems to figure out which is the *cause* and which is the *effect*, people often use the analogy of the chicken and the egg. Which one comes first?

Mental health professionals may wrestle this poultry-sorting question when trying to discern whether an anxiety disorder is causing additional physical or mental health concerns or whether the other physical or mental health issues are producing the symptoms of anxiety.

For example, I commonly see anxiety in my patients who have been diagnosed with irritable bowel syndrome (IBS). This is a medical condition that causes changes in bowel movements, leading to either diarrhea or constipation. IBS also often causes cramping and physical pain.[1]

As you can imagine, people who struggle with frequent pain, and worry about venturing too far from the nearest bathroom, feel stressed. Researchers have also found elevated rates of IBS in people with generalized anxiety disorder and panic disorder.[2] For some individuals with IBS, doctors prescribe anxiety-relieving medications such as selective serotonin reuptake inhibitors (SSRIs). These medications increase levels of the neurotransmitter serotonin, which is thought to produce feelings of well-being and happiness. SSRIs may also relieve IBS symptoms.[3] In these cases, doctors and mental health providers must ask themselves how to proceed. Should they treat the physical problems, the psychological concerns, or both?

The answer is never straightforward, and it generally depends on the person's unique history. As such, in this chapter I have one primary focus: to help you become an educated consumer of your own mental health treatment by considering what *else* you should discuss with your providers while they're arriving at a diagnosis.

Even if you are facing almost anxiety and not a full-fledged anxiety disorder, you and your doctor should rule out other concerns before assuming that you are facing *only* a psychological issue. For example, medical conditions such as inner-ear problems and thyroid dysfunction can produce anxiety symptoms similar to those from panic disorder or generalized anxiety disorder.[4]

As you read this chapter, I encourage you to consider any role that physical problems may potentially be playing in your symptoms before you begin addressing your almost anxiety.

The ABCs of My Anxiety

The first step in accurately diagnosing other possible causes for your feelings of almost anxiety is to consider the **A**ntecedents (what came before) of your **B**ehavior, and the **C**onsequences of a behavior that bothers you. In other words, the **ABCs**.

Let's use an example of something that most of us can easily understand: eating a cookie. Sometimes you might eat a cookie because you are just craving the cookie. Other times, you might be feeling almost anxious, and you find that rewarding yourself with a cookie helps tame your anxiety. Alternatively, you might just be distracted while working on a project and notice that without thinking about it, you have just eaten three large cookies.

The behavior is the same in each situation: you ate cookies. But each situation had a different antecedent (craving, anxiety, distraction), any of which can lead to different emotional consequences—from guilt to contentment—depending on your history and attitudes related to food. Take a few minutes to answer the questions in exercise 3, which will help you untangle any medical and psychological factors contributing to your almost anxiety. You can also download this exercise at www.AlmostAnxious.com.

Exercise 3.
ABCs of Anxiety Questionnaire

1. *What is the primary focus of my anxiety?* In other words, what are you most concerned will happen as a result of your increased anxiety state? Keep in mind that you might be concerned about several of these examples, but try to pinpoint which one is most prominent for you.

   I am concerned about these aspects:

   ☐ uncontrollable worries

   ☐ depression related to anxiety

   ☐ social fears

   ☐ panic-like sensations

   ☐ health-related issues

   ☐ relationship problems

   ☐ family problems

   ☐ drinking or other drug abuse

   ☐ other: _____

2. *When did I first notice that my anxiety had reached a bothersome level?*

   _____

   _____

   _____

3. *What was going on in my life during this time that might have contributed to my heightened anxiety level?* Were there any major changes in your life that might account for your increased anxiety? Keep in mind that even positive changes like having a baby can lead to a temporary jump in your baseline anxiety level.[5] Below are examples of a few stressors that might account for your heightened anxiety:

   ☐ job stressors

   ☐ family stressors

☐ relocation
☐ relationship stressors
☐ financial stressors
☐ loss of support system
☐ death of a loved one
☐ major physical illnesses
☐ other: _____

4. *What makes my anxiety symptoms better?*
☐ exercising
☐ hanging out with friends
☐ eating healthy
☐ relaxing
☐ taking time for myself
☐ taking a mental vacation
☐ meditating
☐ other: _____

5. *What makes my anxiety symptoms worse?*
☐ conflict with my loved ones
☐ demanding tasks at work/home
☐ lack of emotional/physical support
☐ alcohol and drug use
☐ excessive caffeine consumption
☐ lack of restful sleep
☐ unhealthy eating habits
☐ other: _____

6. *Why now?* One of the questions I often ask people when they first come to see me is "Why now?" What was the tipping point that led them to seek help? Give some thought to what drove you to pick up this book and consider tackling your almost anxious state. One way to think about this is to picture how your life would be better if you could learn to manage your anxiety instead of your anxiety running you. So, *why now?*

_____

_____

_____

7. *What are my anxiety-free moments?* When you think of your almost anxious symptoms in the past month, have you had any anxiety-free moments? If so, what did they feel like and what had you been doing during that time?

_____

_____

_____

A close examination of your almost anxiety will help you better understand your own patterns (that is, which factors are antecedents of your behaviors and which are consequences of them) and be able to answer your treatment providers' questions about the course of your almost anxious feelings.

Your answers will also help your providers focus on the true cause of your symptoms. In the event that medical issues are suspected as the cause of your almost anxiety, I'd like to discuss some common medical conditions that mimic anxiety.

Medical Conditions That Can Masquerade as Anxiety

Studies have connected the following health problems with anxiety symptoms. If you have the symptoms of any of these conditions (or have been diagnosed with any of them), it makes sense to consider whether the medical condition may be causing your anxiety symptoms before you and your mental health professional conclude you have almost anxiety. It is important to remember that these conditions are uncommon in the general population. (As a caveat, also keep in mind that you could have any of these conditions *in addition* to almost anxiety.)

- **Labyrinthitis** is an inflammation of the inner ear. When your inner ear is inflamed, you might have balance problems that can lead to dizziness. Dizziness caused by labyrinthitis or other vestibular problems may trigger panic and anxiety symptoms.[6]

- **Mitral valve prolapse (MVP)** is a heart disorder that can cause heart palpitations (rapid heartbeats) and dizziness. MVP may exacerbate panic disorder because it produces feared physical sensations. However, there's some controversy in the medical community as to the nature of the relationship between panic disorder and MVP.[7]

- **Cardiovascular disease** may also cause or exacerbate anxiety with regard to feared physical sensation (such as chest pain). As such, a medical workup for anxiety may include an assessment for cardiovascular illness.

- **Temporal lobe epilepsy** is a brain disorder that creates abnormal electrical activity in the brain's temporal lobe, found at the side of the head. This can also create panic-like symptoms.[8]

- **Pheochromocytoma,** an adrenal gland tumor, can lead to excessive production of adrenaline by the adrenal glands. This in turn can lead to an increase in blood pressure as well as panic-like sensations. Additional symptoms of pheochromocytoma include persistent tachycardia (heart rate exceeding the normal range), weight loss, and blood-pressure spikes.[9]

- **Thyroid disorders.** Both hyperthyroidism (excessive thyroid activity) and hypothyroidism (too-little thyroid activity) can lead to many anxiety-like symptoms, such as nervousness, tremors, and sweating, all of which are also symptoms of generalized anxiety disorder and panic disorder (as well as their almost forms).[10] Other symptoms of hyperthyroidism include weight loss, bulging eyes, persistent tachycardia, and continuous tremors. Other symptoms of hypothyroidism include weight gain, cognitive impairment, hair loss, and skin changes.

- **Irritable bowel syndrome (IBS).** As mentioned earlier, this condition causes diarrhea, constipation, and abdominal pain and cramping. Its cause remains unknown.[11]

To determine whether any of these conditions may be a cause of your almost anxious symptoms or a factor that worsens them, I would recommend that you meet with your primary care physician and have a complete physical exam. My personal policy with patients is to always rule out medical conditions, just to be on the safe side.

This is especially important if you haven't seen your doctor in a while. At the visit, discuss whether you need to rule out some of these conditions with medical assessments, such as a thyroid or heart test. (If it helps relieve any concerns you may have about having a medical condition, all of the almost anxious people I've worked with saw their primary care doctors before coming to see me, and in many cases their medical tests didn't find any physical problems.)

Bring the questionnaire that you completed at the beginning of the chapter to your checkup; it will be very helpful for your doctor as she narrows her focus on a diagnosis.

Psychological Conditions That Can Also Occur alongside Almost Anxiety

Other emotional and mood problems can also fuel almost anxious feelings. For example, researchers estimate that 63 percent of people who are diagnosed with an anxiety disorder also have a depressive disorder.[12] Many of the people I treat who are almost anxious report other emotional difficulties as well:

- Mood and emotional issues can cause anxiety symptoms.
- Anxiety symptoms can cause other psychological problems.
- Anxiety symptoms can occur alongside other mood or emotional issues, without one causing the other.

Again, this can give you a chicken-and-egg conundrum to work out. Here are some common psychological issues that are worth addressing as you're learning how to manage your almost anxiety.

Depression

Symptoms of anxiety and depression—as well as full-fledged anxiety and depressive disorders—frequently occur alongside each other. Researchers estimate that approximately 57 percent of people with major depressive disorder also have an anxiety disorder.[13] Given the high rates of *comorbidity*, meaning the co-occurrence of these conditions, and symptom overlap between anxiety and depression (for example, irritability), the American Psychiatric Association even considered creating a mixed anxiety/depression diagnosis, but ultimately decided against it.[14]

Although there are indeed some similarities between anxiety and depression, research seems to indicate that they are distinct disorders.[15] For example, someone who is primarily facing depressive symptoms is more likely to feel blue and have a lack of energy, while a person who's almost anxious is likely to have "extra" energy and jitteriness. Research suggests that *behavioral activation*, meaning supporting a person in getting re-engaged in life while he or she is depressed, is one way to treat depression.[16] However, when someone is primarily anxious, decreasing the brain chatter is usually called for, which would not be done only by behavioral activation.

If you have both, it's clear that they can be treated simultaneously with cognitive-behavioral therapy, which I'll help you learn to practice throughout this book.

To help determine whether you may also have depression, take a look at the symptoms below. If you have experienced five or more of these symptoms nearly every day in the past two weeks, it's a good idea to ask your doctor or a mental health care provider to screen you for depression.[17] You may also wish to consult *Almost Depressed*, a companion book in this series. Symptoms of depression include

- persistent depressed mood.
- not enjoying things you used to enjoy.

- loss of energy.
- feelings of worthlessness.
- concentration difficulties.
- sleep disturbances.
- feeling sluggish or restless.
- sudden weight gain or loss.
- suicidal thoughts.

Attention Deficit Hyperactivity Disorder (ADHD)

ADHD is an underrecognized and undertreated disorder in adults. Researchers estimate that approximately 12 percent of people with generalized anxiety disorder also have ADHD.[18] Symptoms of this problem can include

- inattention.
- hyperactivity.
- impulsivity.[19]

Adults with ADHD are more likely to experience symptoms of inattention than hyperactivity, and they also report problems with *executive functioning* (such as having trouble planning ahead). ADHD tends to affect all areas of people's lives. That's a contrast to generalized anxiety disorder (GAD), which tends to produce a more focused effect. Both disorders can occur at the same time, and both might warrant treatment.

One step for getting a sense of whether you have generalized anxiety or ADHD is to think about the course of your anxiety. Almost all individuals with ADHD develop the disorder in childhood or adolescence, whereas anxiety disorders can develop anytime throughout adulthood.[20]

Eating Disorders

Eating disorders, such as anorexia and bulimia, are often related to anxiety. Researchers estimate that approximately two-thirds of people with an eating disorder have a current or lifetime history of an anxiety disorder. In addition, the anxiety disorder typically occurs before the development of the eating problem.[21]

Given the strong relationship between disordered eating and anxiety, it is important to consider the focus of your almost anxiety. Do you overeat or undereat when you are anxious? Do your worries center primarily on weight and shape concerns? Eating disorders are serious psychological problems that can be fatal. If you are restricting your food intake or engaging in behaviors such as vomiting or taking laxatives to hold down your weight, you should seek a medical consultation as soon as possible. The good news is that cognitive-behavioral therapy has proven highly effective for the combined treatment of anxiety and eating disorders. If you suspect that disordered eating behaviors may be playing a role in your anxiety symptoms and you'd like to learn more, you can consult *Almost Anorexic*, another book in this series.

Substance Use and Abuse

Alcohol and drug abuse in conjunction with anxiety disorders have been extensively researched. Studies suggest that people with social fears often self-medicate by drinking or using other drugs to reduce the anxiety associated with their fears.[22]

However, in my clinical practice I have also had patients tell me the opposite. Specifically, some patients with social anxiety say that they abstain from alcohol because of the fear of losing control or looking foolish while intoxicated.

Regardless of the relationship between substance use and anxiety symptoms, I often recommend that my patients keep track of their anxiety after using alcohol or other drugs. Heavy drinking is associated with withdrawal symptoms that can mimic anxiety, such as shakiness, irritability, tachycardia, and hypertension.[23] Drugs like caffeine, methamphetamine, and cocaine can also cause shakiness and other symptoms of panic disorder.[24]

If you notice an increase in anxiety symptoms after drinking or using other drugs, it might be prudent to either cut back or stop your substance use while you tackle your almost anxiety. If you suspect that alcohol or drug use may be playing a role in your anxiety symptoms and you'd like to learn more, you can consult *Almost Alcoholic* and *Almost Addicted*, which are companion books in this series. And the best option when you suspect that your drinking or drug use is causing a problem is to consult with your primary care physician or see an addiction counselor for an assessment.

Hypochondriasis

Nowadays known as "health anxiety," this is a condition in which people often feel worried that they might have a serious medical condition, like cancer or AIDS. Even after seeking multiple medical opinions and receiving a clean bill of physical health, people with health anxiety often have a difficult time believing that their symptoms, such as tingling in the extremities or racing heartbeat, are caused by their anxiety rather than a medical condition.

Health anxiety and the other anxiety disorders share some

symptoms (such as worry about health-related problems). However, I will not specifically address health anxiety in this book. If you believe you have health anxiety, I would recommend consulting with a mental health professional, seeking out literature specific to health anxiety, or doing both. That being said, individuals with health anxiety may also be almost anxious in other areas, as they might worry about issues such as social events that are not related to their health anxiety. If that is the case for you, read on to learn how you can better manage your worries.

I have highlighted the most common disorders that can mimic almost anxiety or coexist with it, but this list is not exhaustive. Again, it's best to discuss your symptoms with your doctor, as my patients who are almost anxious have done. This visit may uncover important health concerns that you should address, and it may give you new tools for reducing your almost anxiety.

• • •

Now that you have a good understanding of why it's important to manage your almost anxiety, let's take a closer look at your particular symptoms. Almost anxiety comes in different "flavors," and coming to terms with this problem requires knowing which type you have.

◆

Part 2

Learning about Your Anxiety

4

What's Your Almost Anxious Flavor?

As the waiters cleared away our dessert plates, the conversation between my colleagues and me heated up. We were attending an annual conference, and our thoughts turned to the upcoming changes to our diagnostic system, the *DSM*. As I noted earlier, this is the manual published by the American Psychiatric Association that sets the diagnostic criteria for mental health disorders; it is updated periodically to account for new research. At that point, it was in transition from its then-current version to the version we use now, *DSM-5*.

We debated with each other: "Should the criteria for generalized anxiety disorder be changed? If so, how? Should it require only three months of chronic excessive worry instead of the accepted six months? How about obsessive-compulsive disorder? Should it remain under the umbrella of 'anxiety disorders,' or should it be moved to its own category?"

Many of us had direct experience researching these issues or were involved with groups that did such work, so we felt strongly about our views. Although the conversation was amicable, I felt like I was participating in a presidential debate, with emotions running high as we all wanted our side to "win."

Growing up in small-town Brazil, I had never dreamed of hanging around in circles where decisions were made that would affect my entire profession. As I walked home that night, I wasn't sure if the "buzz" I felt was because my brain was titillated by the discussion or by the extra glass of wine I'd had during dinner.

In Brazil, there is a belief that if you have had too much to drink, you should have an espresso to sober up. After a week of feeling academically tipsy from my meeting, my espresso arrived in the form of a new patient, Christian. He was a lanky, out-and-proud gay Asian man in his late forties who arrived impeccably dressed for our first meeting. I still recall his pink tie.

Christian was one strong shot of espresso! I was immediately sobered and brought back down to earth from my academic exercises, as I was reminded what these intellectual concepts actually mean in terms of emotional pain in people's lives in the real world.

Christian's Story

Christian was bearing the burden of anxiety (I hadn't determined yet whether he was almost anxious or had a full-blown anxiety disorder), and he was more than ready for relief. In our initial evaluation, I irritated him as I attempted to pick apart his specific symptoms.

"Doctor, it is *all* anxiety! I don't care if you call it social fears, worry, or panic; I'm telling you, it's just plain anxiety," he explained. "I need help because my boyfriend is getting tired of it. He hates seeing me anxious, and lately I can't seem to bring it down. Last week, I did six CrossFit workouts, which is double my usual, and I was still feeling *anxious*. Honestly, I am not interested in taking your quizzes to figure out my anxiety type. I just want help!"

Christian was not—and will not be—the last patient I treat who becomes impatient while I'm analyzing his or her experience of anxiety. When folks first come to see me, they want immediate help, whether they have full-blown anxiety or are almost anxious. By the time people make a decision to see a professional, it usually means they're uncomfortable in their lives, and the last thing they want is for someone to examine them like a lab rat.

But to mental health professionals, finding the correct diagnosis is key to providing the correct treatment. You've already learned how to determine whether you are almost anxious, which falls between normal, healthy levels of anxiety and full-blown anxiety disorders (recall the spectrum pictured in figure 2).

But almost anxiety is not just a single concept. It comes in different "flavors": worry, social, and physical (see figure 5). The box in this figure illustrates Christian's experience of anxiety: it was one large, uncomfortable feeling that was negatively affecting his life. I tried to understand whether Christian's experience was highlighted more by

- general worries
- fearfulness in social situations
- discomfort with physical sensations

These are the smaller circles within the almost anxiety box. The more questions I asked, the more I understood that Christian's experience was a mixture of the almost anxious subtypes. Christian was worrying most of the time, but his anxiety was particularly pronounced when he had a meeting with his boss.

Figure 5.
The Anxiety Flavors

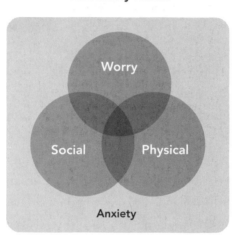

Why would you want to determine the precise flavors of your anxiety experience? Why not just call it almost anxiety and move on to figuring out how to reduce it?

Because when you know which subtype (or types) of almost anxiety you have, you can better understand how you get "stuck" in your almost anxious feelings (the focus of chapter 5) and how to best tackle those feelings. For example, if you experience more social fears, you might tend to get stuck more on avoiding parties or important presentations. On the other hand, if you are in the worry subtype, then you might always be in your head *thinking* about everything (including your own thoughts!) and feeling emotionally stuck with an overall sense of stress and worry. If you have more of the physical subtype, you might avoid things not because they are scary socially, like parties, but because you are concerned you might develop panic-like sensations in those situations.

Although one of the almost anxious subtypes might be more prominent than the others for you, many people I treat experience anxiety from all of the subtypes. The main goal of this chapter is to help you identify your primary flavor and get a more nuanced sense of how your almost anxiety manifests itself. Let's start by exploring the worry subtype.

Almost Anxious: Worry Type

Worry is a natural process that most of us experience. It can help us tend to important obligations in our lives. For example, someone might worry about fixing up his or her house before trying to sell it to bring in the highest possible bid on it. In this case, worry has a valuable purpose. Similarly, the process of worrying can indicate that you need to do more planning, such as worrying about getting your passport renewed for an upcoming overseas trip, which takes time to complete. As long as the worry propels you to move forward or it's only momentary, it is not necessarily a bad thing. However, worry crosses the peak of the performance curve and moves into the almost spectrum when it starts to interfere with your life.

Your worry may have crossed into the almost anxious zone if you meet the following criteria:

- excessive worries for a period of at least three months
- worries that are not due to specific stressful situations (like losing your job)

- worries that interfere with at least one area of your life (such as family, friends, or significant others; work or other professional areas; or emotional factors such as self-esteem)

The Penn State Worry Questionnaire (PSWQ) is another tool that can help you determine whether you fall within the almost anxious worry subtype. The PSWQ is a measure of generalized anxiety and worry. Scores on the PSWQ range from 16 to 80.[1]

Take a few minutes to answer the questions in exercise 4, or download the questionnaire at www.AlmostAnxious.com. Thinking about your worry *for the past three months*, rate each of the following statements from 1 ("not at all typical of me") to 5 ("very typical of me").

To tally up your PSWQ score, you will need to score the items marked with an asterisk (*) in reverse. That's because the total score is supposed to indicate *higher* worries, but for some questions, such as "If I do *not* have enough time to do everything, I do *not* worry about it," a high score of 5 would mean that you do not worry much.

So reverse the values you wrote down for questions 1, 3, 8, 10, and 11. In other words, switch 1s to 5s and vice versa, 2s to 4s and vice versa. A score of 3 remains the same. After you reverse the scores for these questions, then add up the results for all the sixteen questions to get your total score.

Here's what the scores indicate:

- From 16 to 45 points, you have normal levels of worry.
- From 46 to 67, you fall within the almost anxious spectrum.

Exercise 4.

The Penn State Worry Questionnaire

Not at all typical of me				Very typical of me	
1	2	3	4	5	My Score
1. If I do not have enough time to do everything, I do not worry about it.*					
2. My worries overwhelm me.					
3. I do not tend to worry about things.*					
4. Many situations make me worry.					
5. I know I should not worry about things, but I just cannot help it.					
6. When I am under pressure, I worry a lot.					
7. I am always worrying about something.					
8. I find it easy to dismiss worrisome thoughts.*					
9. As soon as I finish one task, I start to worry about everything else I have to do.					
10. I never worry about anything.*					
11. When there is nothing more I can do about a concern, I do not worry about it anymore.*					
12. I have been a worrier all my life.					
13. I notice that I have been worrying about things.					
14. Once I start worrying, I cannot stop.					
15. I worry all the time.					
16. I worry about projects until they are all done.					

- 68 or above, you may want to consider visiting a mental health provider to discuss your symptoms.

Almost Anxious: Social Type

Much like worrying, feeling concerned with how people perceive you during social situations is normal.

Although I had known most of the colleagues I was dining with at that mental health conference for years, I was still a little self-conscious about participating in that conversation. Some are leaders in my field, and I'd prefer them to have a good impression of me!

So I tried to choose my words carefully. This is not different from the experience of people going to a job interview, a first date, or a first visit with their future in-laws. After all, just about everyone wants to be liked by others. Having mild levels of social fear in appropriate social settings without being avoidant is a normal part of human experience.

Yet in the anxiety spectrum, there may come a time when you travel over the peak of the anxiety curve, and your social concern becomes too much and starts to interfere with your life. You may be almost anxious with the social subtype if

- you avoid social situations that are anxiety provoking.

- avoidance leads to interference in at least one area of your life, such as with your family, friends, or significant others; your professional life; or your emotions.

Much like the worry questionnaire you worked through earlier, a quiz is available to help you determine whether your social fears may be falling within the almost range. It's called the Social Phobia Inventory, also known as the SPIN.

The SPIN is a brief measure of social anxiety symptoms. It assesses a variety of problems such as fear of social situations (like talking to strangers), avoidance of social situations (like going to parties), and physical symptoms (like blushing).[2]

Scores on this inventory range from 0 to 68, with higher scores indicating more social anxiety symptoms.

Since the idea of almost anxiety is a new concept, I relied on many studies that measured SPIN scores in different groups of people to determine a range of scores that would suggest your social fears have entered the almost anxious area.

Please take a few minutes to complete the SPIN in exercise 5. Or download the exercise at www.AlmostAnxious.com.

Based on research data, I recommend the following guide for categorizing your score:[3]

- From 0 to 15 points, you likely fall within the normal levels of social fears.
- From 16 to 28, you are within the almost anxious social subtype.
- 29 or above, you should consider contacting a mental health professional to be evaluated for social anxiety disorder.

Almost Anxious: Physical Type

Usually when primary care doctors ask me to consult on a case, it's because their patients are reporting physical symptoms of anxiety, such as heart pounding, sweating, dizziness, and difficulty breathing. Usually, the doctor has put the patient through a battery of medical tests that have found nothing, led to inconclusive results, or indicated a combination of a medical and emotional problem, with an anxiety flavor.

Exercise 5.

Social Phobia Inventory

Indicate how much the following problems have bothered you during the *past week*. Choose only one number for each problem, and be sure to answer all of the items. Please rate each question using the following scale ranging from 0 ("not at all") to 4 ("extremely").

Not at all	A little	Somewhat	Very much	Extremely	
0	1	2	3	4	My Score
1.	I am afraid of people in authority.				
2.	I am bothered by blushing in front of people.				
3.	Parties and social events scare me.				
4.	I avoid talking to people I don't know.				
5.	Being criticized scares me a lot.				
6.	Fear of embarrassment causes me to avoid doing things or speaking in public.				
7.	Sweating in front of people causes me distress.				
8.	I avoid going to parties.				
9.	I avoid activities in which I am the center of attention.				
10.	Talking to strangers scares me.				
11.	I avoid having to give speeches.				
12.	I would do anything to avoid being criticized.				
13.	Heart palpitations bother me when I am around people.				
14.	I am afraid of doing things when people might be watching.				
15.	Being embarrassed or looking stupid is among my worst fears.				
16.	I avoid speaking to anyone in authority.				
17.	Trembling or shaking in front of others is distressing to me.				
Total score (sum of all scores)					

Regardless of the outcome, the doctor usually wants me to teach the patient how to manage physical symptoms of anxiety. You already know that anxiety is helpful up to a point, so "managing" doesn't equal "completely getting rid of" anxiety.

But as with other flavors of almost anxiety, even just a little too much of the physical subtype can be uncomfortable. As you cross over into being almost anxious with the physical subtype, you'll notice these symptoms:

- repetitive and intrusive fear of having panic-like sensations
- avoidance of places, people, or situations that might induce these physical anxiety sensations
- avoidance that interferes with at least one area of your life: interpersonal, professional, or emotional

A quiz that's useful for identifying the physical subtype of almost anxiety is the Hospital Anxiety and Depression Scale —Anxiety Subscale (HADS-A), presented in exercise 6 and available at www.AlmostAnxious.com. This quiz measures both physical symptoms of anxiety (like panic) and the subjective symptoms of anxiety (like feeling terrified). Scores on the HADS-A range from 0 to 21.[4]

The authors of the scale suggested that a score between 8 and 10 was on the border between no diagnosis and diagnosis for an anxiety disorder. Other researchers have used cutoff scores as low as 3 or as high as 11 to screen for "diagnosable" anxiety symptoms.[5] I present an interpretation of different score ranges below. However, if your score is greater than 8, you may want to consult a mental health professional to rule out a diagnosis.

Exercise 6.

Hospital Anxiety and Depression Scale—Anxiety Subscale

Read each item and circle the reply that comes closest to how you have been feeling in the past week.

		My Score
1.	I feel tense or "wound up":	
	- Most of the time	3
	- A lot of the time	2
	- From time to time, occasionally	1
	- Not at all	0
2.	I get a sort of frightened feeling as if something awful is about to happen:	
	- Very definitely and quite badly	3
	- Yes, but not too badly	2
	- A little, but it doesn't worry me	1
	- Not at all	0
3.	Worrying thoughts go through my mind:	
	- A great deal of the time	3
	- A lot of the time	2
	- From time to time, but not too often	1
	- Only occasionally	0
4.	I can sit at ease and feel relaxed:	
	- Definitely	3
	- Usually	2
	- Not often	1
	- Not at all	0

		My Score
5.	I get a sort of frightened feeling like "butterflies" in my stomach:	
	- Not at all	3
	- Occasionally	2
	- Quite often	1
	- Very often	0
6.	I feel restless, as if I have to be on the move:	
	- Very much indeed	3
	- Quite a lot	2
	- Not very much	1
	- Not at all	0
7.	I get a sudden feeling of panic:	
	- Very often indeed	3
	- Quite often	2
	- Not very often	1
	- Not at all	0
Total score (sum of your scores for each of the items)		

Here's what the scores indicate:

- From 0 to 7 points, you appear to have healthy levels of physical anxiety sensations.
- From 8 to 10, you appear to have the almost anxious physical subtype.
- 11 or above, please consider visiting a mental health professional to rule out a diagnosis of panic disorder or another anxiety disorder.

Christian's Outcome

Despite Christian's protests, I coaxed him into taking these quizzes so we could get a better sense of his experience with anxiousness (which he'd initially described as "just anxiety").

When Christian completed the PSWQ to check for the "worry" type of anxiety, he had a total score of 46, which is in the lower end of the almost spectrum for worries. When we discussed it, Christian explained that his worries had been elevated lately—mostly because he was concerned that his boyfriend might leave him due to his anxiety—but that he would not have described himself as a worrier. "I am a happy man, Doc, with lots of friends and a full social life," he said. "If it weren't for worrying uncontrollably about Marcelo leaving me, I would not be fretting. Life is too short to fret."

We moved on to the SPIN quiz to measure his feelings of anxiety in social situations. Here his score was a 25, indicating that his social fear fell within the almost anxious social spectrum. Christian had described a full social life, with biweekly dinner parties at his condo and frequent trips to the best restaurants, jazz clubs, and weekend hot spots in Boston. His surprisingly high score intrigued me. "What caused *that*?" I wondered.

Was his almost anxiety truly more of the social type, but he had found ways around it by having a close group of friends with whom he felt comfortable? Or did the questions about physical concerns in the social quiz, like question 13 about heart palpitations around other people, bump up his score?

His answers on the HADS-A, a measure of physical symptoms, were very illuminating. Christian's score was the most elevated in the HADS-A, with a score of 8, which put him almost at a diagnosis of an anxiety disorder, but still within the range of almost anxious, physical type. Christian indeed was experiencing a lot of panic-like symptoms, which were bothering him plenty. Christian's boyfriend was also frustrated that Christian was starting to change his behaviors in response to his physical symptoms. For example, Christian was having a lot of stomach problems and gastrointestinal discomfort, which had limited their dinner parties and social engagements, both of which Marcelo found annoying. (It is not the symptoms per se that were upsetting Marcelo; it was Christian's initial reluctance to seek help.)

Take-Home Lessons from the Anxiety Quizzes

Christian's experience illustrates why I find it extremely important to examine the different flavors of being almost anxious. If he hadn't taken all three quizzes, I may have had difficulty narrowing down the precise issues contributing to his discomfort.

Your results from these quizzes can also be illuminating. I hope that by completing these quizzes, you were able to get a sense of how your own almost anxiety manifests and where you fall within the different flavors. Figure 6 shows a quick summary of what the scores indicate.

Figure 6.
Summary of Scores for Almost Anxious Flavors:
Worry (PSWQ), Social (SPIN), and Physical (HADS-A)

	Normal Mood	Almost Anxious	Full-Blown Anxiety Disorders
PSWQ:	16–45	46–67	68+
SPIN:	0–15	16–28	29+
HADS–A	0–7	8–10	11+

Giving Deeper Thought to Your Almost Anxiety Flavor(s)

Christian initially didn't see much reason to delve into the particulars of his anxious symptoms. To him, anxiety was anxiety, and he merely wanted less of it.

But carefully exploring his symptoms helped him and me understand and then treat his case. Christian and I made what experts call a "fine-grain analysis" of each item on the three scales to better understand the factors contributing to his worry, social anxiety, and physical symptoms.

This more detailed look showed us that Christian was not much of a worrier. And while he appeared to have problems in social settings, these results actually pointed to physical concerns of anxiety that could play out in social interactions. Namely, Christian scored high on these SPIN questions:

- I am bothered by *blushing* in front of people.
- *Sweating* in front of people causes me distress.
- *Heart palpitations* bother me when I am around people.
- *Trembling or shaking* in front of others is distressing to me.

This is not uncommon, and it may explain why many people think of anxiety and almost anxiety as one overwhelming, all-encompassing symptom. The important question here is: "What is driving my symptoms?" Christian was afraid not of social situations per se but of the possibility of experiencing physical symptoms during those interactions. Review each answer on your three quizzes, and compare and contrast them, in addition to noticing which items you scored higher on.

Figure 7.
Summary of Christian's Scores across Anxiety Flavors

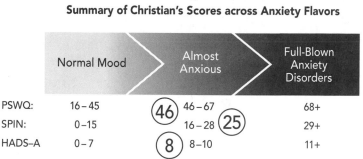

	Normal Mood	Almost Anxious	Full-Blown Anxiety Disorders
PSWQ:	16–45	(46) 46–67 (25)	68+
SPIN:	0–15	16–28	29+
HADS–A	0–7	(8) 8–10	11+

Using Your Anxiety Flavor to Tackle Your Almost Anxious Feelings

One of the advantages of really knowing how you experience almost anxiety is that you'll be better equipped to tackle it.

For example, when Christian and I started to work on cognitive-behavioral therapy skills (which you'll learn in part 3 of this book), we didn't focus much on his worry or his feelings during social situations. Instead, we targeted his physical symptoms by exposing him to some of his feared sensations; for example, he ran up and down a staircase to induce sweating.

But we didn't completely neglect the scores on the social quiz, either. We knew that social situations were one area in which Christian experienced some bothersome physical symptoms. So I encouraged him to stop avoiding these situations and instead approach them with the expectation that he would have the sensations. Although the process of therapy for Christian might be different from yours, knowing your anxiety flavor will undoubtedly shape the treatment that you receive. (It's a bit like knowing the precise bacteria that's causing an infection in order to choose the most appropriate antibiotic.)

No matter how you experience almost anxiety, you can get stuck in your symptoms—whether they're worry, social, or physical. When Christian came into my office for the first time, I think this is what he was trying to tell me: "I am stuck in a cycle of anxiety that I can't seem to manage." Next, we'll pull out the "hamster wheel" and learn how your brain can get stuck in a cycle of fear.

■ ◆ ■

5

Step Off the Almost Anxious Hamster Wheel

A common feature in hamster cages is the hamster wheel. You've probably seen one of these stationary wheels, which is the rodent version of a treadmill. The faster the hamster runs, the faster the wheel spins beneath its feet. But the faster the wheel spins, the more quickly the little creature has to pump its feet to keep up. People with almost anxiety are likely to get stuck in a cycle that's very similar to this, which I call the Almost Anxious Hamster Wheel (figure 8). This is a common experience among the patients I work with:

Their almost anxiety causes unpleasant physical sensations or emotions such as fear, leading them to . . .

. . . avoid certain situations (behavior), which causes them to have . . .

. . . negative thoughts about themselves, which triggers . . .

. . . more physical sensations and unpleasant emotions.

Eventually, hamsters hop off their exercise wheel and find other things to do with their time. You, too, can step off your almost anxious wheel when it starts spinning. But before I talk about how you can make your exit, I'd like to show you an example of how people can set their wheel in motion.

Figure 8.
The Almost Anxious Hamster Wheel

Jonathan's Story

Jonathan was a teacher in his early sixties who worked in an urban school. He had spent years working with children and adolescents with challenging home lives. I immediately felt a sense of ease during my first session with Jonathan; he carried himself in a calm, cool, respectful manner. I sensed that he displayed this demeanor around his students too.

Jonathan said he often felt a little overwhelmed with the demands of balancing his home duties as a father and husband with being the best teacher he could be, which was an important aspect of his life.

Despite the daily stressors, Jonathan felt that he could manage his multiple demands while maintaining an upbeat attitude. However, this all changed when he came upon a "once in a lifetime" career opportunity. (Even happy situations can set the almost anxious wheel spinning underneath our feet.)

Throughout Jonathan's career, he had developed a special curriculum for distressed children that helped them approach their emotional difficulties while they were engaging in academics. Jonathan's school principal, Mario, approached him about sharing the curriculum with other inner-city schools around the country. The two men had worked together closely for nearly twenty years, and Mario had been one of Jonathan's biggest cheerleaders. The principal had seen firsthand the impact of Jonathan's program on the students' academic success and emotional well-being, and word about the program's benefits had spread to other school districts.

But the idea of promoting the program created a significant emotional roadblock for Jonathan, which brought him to my office. With tears in his eyes, Jonathan said, "My life is perfect! I love my job, my wife and kids, and my friends. I get immense satisfaction from seeing my students, who have significant trauma in their personal lives, find ways to succeed while avoiding violence and drugs. I truly feel honored that I get to impact their lives so much."

Then he got to the problem that was propelling his almost anxious wheel into motion. "I should be thrilled that Mario would want me to take the lead on bringing our curriculum to other schools, but instead I am terrified, scared, and paralyzed. I can't stop thinking about what that would mean!"

Jonathan pictured himself walking into large auditoriums to give presentations to educators about his program, then seeing himself running away because he couldn't think of words to say. "I don't know where this is coming from. I have always been mildly uncomfortable with public speaking, but never to this extent. I have given smaller versions of this talk to *hundreds* of educators, so I ask myself why this would be a problem," he told me. "I'll be retiring in a few years and I know this is an important thing for me to do, especially at this point in my career. I want to leave a legacy. But the minute I picture myself in this new role, my heart pounds, I start to sweat, and I immediately want to tell Mario to forget about it. I am stuck. What should I do?"

Thoughts, Feelings, and Behaviors on the Almost Anxious Wheel

To help Jonathan find an answer to that question, I began by telling him about the anxiety hamster wheel. Again, the wheel has three main pieces: thoughts, feelings, and behaviors.

- **Thoughts** are the things you tell yourself. In other words, these are the words and sentences you form in your head.

- **Feelings** include emotions (like fear, sadness, and happiness) and physical sensations (like heart pounding or muscle tension). For simplicity's sake, we are going to group them all together as "feelings" on the almost anxious wheel.

- **Behaviors** include your actions and inactions. The most common behavior in the wheel is *avoidance*.

The first step in getting unstuck from this cycle of anxious thoughts, strong emotions, and unhelpful anxiety-management behaviors is to identify the precise thoughts, feelings, and behaviors that feed your anxiety. This task is not as easy as it sounds. Indeed, it has been a struggle for nearly every almost anxious patient I have ever treated. In particular, it can be hard to tell the difference between the parts of the anxiety wheel. Even so, it is critical to do so. *The ability to identify the thoughts, feelings, and behaviors that fuel your anxiety will provide the foundation for each subsequent step of successfully addressing your almost anxiety.* As such, I would strongly urge you to spend plenty of time working through this chapter and developing a thorough understanding of how your almost anxious wheel is put together.

Distinguishing between Thoughts, Feelings, and Behaviors

Many people who are almost anxious confuse how they are feeling (sad and fearful) with their thoughts ("Something is wrong with me"). When I ask my patients, "What were you *thinking* about right before your presentation?" (or other upsetting situation), I often hear answers like these:

- "I was *feeling* anxious, scared, and fearful."
- "My heart was pounding; I was sweaty and slightly nauseated."
- "I was *feeling* embarrassed, like I was about to humiliate myself."
- "I wanted to run away from the stage."

Have you ever had these "thoughts"?

Most people, even those who are comfortable giving public presentations, have had things cross their minds during stressful situations that sound a lot like what Jonathan described to me. Which are the *thoughts*, which are the *feelings*, and which are the *behaviors*? When you're in the midst of this situation, they can be hard to separate.

In Jonathan's case, the following exchange helped him learn to separate his thoughts from his feelings and behaviors.

Dr. M.: Jonathan, what is the first *thought* that comes to your mind when you think about giving a presentation on your curriculum in front of representatives from numerous school districts?

Jonathan: I feel anxious, scared, and overwhelmed. My heart skips a beat, and I am slightly nauseated, perhaps also a little light-headed. It makes it hard for me to concentrate. (*He looked pale and slightly anxious even describing this experience.*)

Dr. M.: So it sounds like when you picture yourself on that stage, you start to experience a lot of bodily sensations, much like you would have in a fight-or-flight experience, like an increase in your heart rate, a sense of nausea, and light-headedness. Right?

Jonathan: Yes, I can literally feel my heart skip a beat and then it begins to pound as loud as a drum. I swear I can hear it!

Dr. M.: This sounds really uncomfortable! But it also sounds like you experience some feelings associated with these sensations. Can you separate them from each other?

Jonathan: Feelings? I guess I feel scared and anxious; that is why I want to run away from the stage. It is very uncomfortable.

Dr. M.: I'll bet! It sounds like your body gets a major adrenaline rush, causing the physical sensations associated with the image of you giving this presentation. As a result, you really want to *do* something to stop those physical sensations. It sounds like you've come up with a *behavior* to solve this problem: you want to *run away* from the stage. That makes a lot of sense to me. If you were to run away, then it is likely that your body might calm down and you would immediately feel a sense of relief, right?

Jonathan: I hadn't thought about it that way, but I guess it makes sense. I do see myself running away from the stage, and I get a sense of relief. *(He has a gloomy look on his face now.)*

Dr. M.: Jonathan, I'm confused. You just told me that running away would be associated with a sense of relief, and yet you look sad. Were you *feeling* sad?

Jonathan: *(Tears are now running from his eyes.)* Yes! I started to feel like a loser, a failure, an impostor. If I can't do this, why is it that I worked so hard for so many years to develop and test this curriculum? I must be a failure.

Dr. M.: Wow . . . Those are really upsetting *thoughts*! It sounds like the physical relief you might have felt if you ran away from the stage would only have lasted a second, and then you would immediately experience a lot of thoughts related to what you did. I am hearing that you would say to yourself the following things: "I am a loser . . . I am an impostor . . . I am a failure." Is that correct?

Jonathan: *(Still tearing up.)* Yes, I guess I would be saying those things to myself, again and again . . . .

Dr. M.: Jonathan, how would those thoughts impact you? How do you think they would make you feel?

Jonathan: I would have felt sad, disappointed in myself, anxious, and slightly terrified. I guess I would have felt embarrassed too.

Dr. M.: I can see how those thoughts would lead to those feelings. I am curious, what is the *thought* that might be related to the *feeling* of being embarrassed?

Jonathan: I guess I was *thinking* that people would think that *I am a loser*, and that would make me *feel* really *embarrassed*.

Dr. M.: That is it! You got it, Jonathan. You just separated what you were saying to yourself, your thoughts, from what you were *feeling*.

After our exchange, Jonathan's anxiety wheel looked like figure 9.

Figure 9.
Almost Anxious Wheel, Social Type

Almost Anxious Wheel: Social Type

Jonathan is a great example of someone with the social type of almost anxiety. Cognitive-behavioral therapists believe that individuals with social anxiety generate negative *thoughts* about how they appear to others.[1] These negative thoughts lead them to feel anxious and distressed in social situations and to behave in a way that minimizes these emotions, either by avoiding social situations or by employing safety behaviors (like not making eye contact). In this way, people with social anxiety never learn that most social situations are not threatening. This example illustrates the wheel for the social type of almost anxiety.

Almost Anxious Wheel: Worry Type

With the worry type of almost anxiety, people often get stuck "thinking about thinking." Studies suggest that worrying helps us avoid emotions.[2] In essence, researchers noted that by worrying nonstop, people can avoid the *other* emotions that stressful events can trigger. For example, when faced with the need to work on an important project, someone with almost anxiety might fixate on the wording of a particular email, worrying about how to make it perfect, instead of actually taking action on the project. By worrying about worrying, the person might (temporarily) avoid feeling upset. However, as time passes, irritability, edginess, and frustration likely break through the worry.

Another reason that people tend to continually worry long-term is their belief that doing so helps them solve problems or prevent bad outcomes. However, this mind-set is a recipe for disaster, since the catastrophes people fear rarely happen. And making this problem worse, they constantly reinforce their superstitious belief that worry *prevents* these outcomes.

In reality, worrying actually increases the perceived threat and uncontrollability of feared outcomes rather than prevent them. You can see how people might find themselves stuck in an endless cycle of worrying! To illustrate this point, let's consider how a mother might worry about her child leaving home for college (figure 10). This is an example I often hear in my practice.

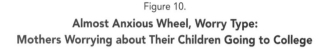

Figure 10.
Almost Anxious Wheel, Worry Type:
Mothers Worrying about Their Children Going to College

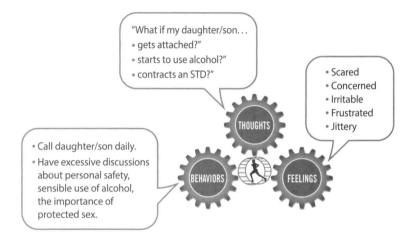

Similar to Jonathan with his work presentations, mothers—and fathers—with these thoughts can get stuck in the almost anxious wheel. The more they worry, the more upsetting feelings they are likely to have, which they might try to manage by engaging in any of the behaviors I've described.

The problem here is that parents do not have much control over what happens to their children while they're in college. Their effort to control their kids' safety is in vain, leading to even more worry. Moreover, their constant nagging might even create a self-fulfilling prophecy—for example, their kids ignore their parents' annoying check-in calls or they drink more alcohol than they otherwise would because their parents imbued it with an attractive "forbidden" status.

Almost Anxious Wheel: Physical Type

In contrast to the worry subtype, in which people typically step onto the almost anxious wheel through their thinking, those with the bodily subtype tend to notice their physical sensations first. For these people, bodily sensations (such as dizziness from standing up too fast, breathlessness brought on by exercise, or heart palpitations triggered by daily stressors) are interpreted as signs of danger (such as insanity or heart attack). Making such catastrophic misinterpretations of these bodily sensations only leads them to feel more anxious and to experience even more unpleasant bodily sensations.[3]

As the wheel spins, they become more and more anxious and may eventually have a panic attack. People with panic disorder—and even the *almost* form of panic—frequently have heightened levels of what researchers call *anxiety sensitivity*. Anxiety sensitivity is the belief that the experience of anxiety is itself harmful.[4] Negative beliefs about anxiety may prompt such people to avoid situations in which they feel anxious or to employ safety behaviors (such as sitting down) when they feel anxious, resulting in the maintenance of these negative beliefs.

Figure 11 shows what an almost anxious wheel would look like for someone with the physical type of almost anxiety.

Figure 11.
Almost Anxious Wheel, Physical Type

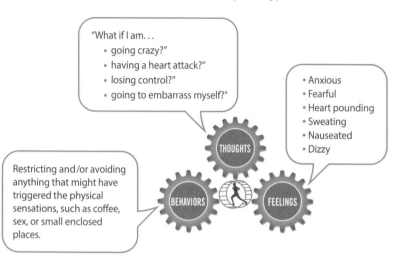

Identifying Your Own Anxiety-Related Thoughts, Feelings and Behaviors

The lessons that Jonathan learned apply to dealing with almost anxiety in general. I often take an approach with my patients that's similar to what I used with Jonathan. Let's explore some points to keep in mind as you begin identifying your own thoughts, feelings, and behaviors.

The Factors in the Wheel Go Round and Round

There were several points in my conversation with Jonathan when a specific thought would lead to a feeling and vice versa. For example, he had the *thought* "I am a failure," and this resulted in the *feeling* of embarrassment. Similarly, he had the *physical sensation* of heart pounding that led him to the thought that he was a failure. Regardless of where you enter the almost anxious wheel—whether by a thought, an emotion or physical sensation, or a behavior to avoid the experience—you might get stuck in this vicious cycle.

Feelings Are Often Confused with Thoughts

I can't emphasize enough the importance of pinpointing whether you're having a feeling, thought, or physical sensation. When I asked Jonathan about his thoughts related to giving a presentation, he responded with *feelings* (scared, anxious) and *physical sensations* (heart pounding, sweating). We had to work together to uncover his actual *thoughts*.

This is not surprising to me. Many languages use "I feel . . ." to describe a thought. For example, Jonathan would say, "I feel like a failure." If you look at the almost anxious wheel, you will notice that this thought quickly triggers his feelings of "anxiety, fear, and sadness." From Jonathan's perspective, he's having them all at the same time.

I would encourage you to have patience with yourself while you learn to pick apart the nuances between your thoughts, feelings, and behaviors. Even after years of experience, I still find myself confusing them at times. This is a skill, and like any other skill you have learned in your life, whether playing the piano or learning how to drive, it takes practice. In cognitive-behavioral therapy, we often say that you only get as much out of therapy as you put into it, and the key is practice, practice, practice!

Putting your thoughts, feelings, and behaviors into your own almost anxious wheel over and over again will help you differentiate between them. To help you practice, consider the list of emotions and physical responses to anxiety in exercise 7. As you can see, most feelings can be described in a single word (like "happy" or "sad"). In contrast, thoughts are more often a phrase or sentence (such as "I am a loser"). Read through the list of examples, and then write down some of your own responses. You can also download this exercise at www .AlmostAnxious.com.

Exercise 7.
Physical and Emotional Responses to Almost Anxiety

Take a few minutes to think back to the last time you felt almost anxious. What physical and emotional responses did you have? Write down your own experience below.

Feelings
Examples: Anxious, embarrassed, scared, frustrated

_____

_____

_____

_____

_____

_____

Physical Sensations
Examples: Blushing, shakiness, a pounding heart, sweating

_____

_____

_____

_____

_____

_____

Exploring Your Feelings to Uncover Your Thoughts

Most people notice when their emotions suddenly change. For example, think about the last time you were sitting at work and the computer made a pinging noise to tell you yet another unwanted email had arrived that needed your attention. Perhaps you started to feel anxious, overwhelmed, and stressed. Or maybe you were discussing monthly bills with your spouse and you began having a sense of doom, as though something bad were about to happen. Our emotional and physical feelings have important evolutionary benefits. They are designed to raise the alert that something is wrong. This is incredibly helpful when you are facing a threat to your life (let's say a lion leaps the fence at the zoo while you're visiting!). But the alert is less helpful when you're simply facing a load of work or a big bill to pay.

A Note for Visual Learners

Some people who are very visual might not experience a clear verbal thought; rather, they might get pictures in their mind. Images like Jonathan's picture of himself bolting from his presentation can elicit emotions and physical sensations as strongly —if not more so—as verbal thoughts can. So if you are visualizing yourself avoiding action, there is likely a thought behind that image that you could work on verbalizing. For example, Jonathan would visualize himself freezing up on stage, which made him think "I am a failure! People will laugh at me! I will embarrass myself!" Who would not feel almost anxious with these thoughts?

When you notice a sudden change in your mood, ask yourself, "What was I telling myself right before my mood changed?" If you draw a blank, try another question: "What does it mean to me when I feel _____ ?" (*Fill in the blank with an emotion: sad, happy, anxious, afraid . . . .*) Similarly, you can ask yourself, "What am I afraid will happen in this situation?" Any of these questions will help you start disentangling your thoughts from your feelings. Again, this is a skill, and you will need to practice it to become good at it.

As a person who is fairly attuned to her feelings but pays much less attention to her thoughts, I can assure you that if I learned how to do this, so can you! Begin by identifying some of your thoughts in exercise 8; you can also download this exercise at www.AlmostAnxious.com.

Exercise 8.
Thoughts Wheel

Recalling a time when you were anxious, identify some of your thoughts at that time. (If you get stuck, these thoughts might help you brainstorm: "I can't control my thoughts." "I will embarrass myself." "People will make fun of me." "I am having a heart attack." "I will lose control and go crazy.") Now list some of your own anxious thoughts:

_____

_____

_____

_____

_____

_____

_____

When you notice a sudden change in your feelings, ask yourself any of the following questions to pinpoint the thought(s) that might be triggering your almost anxious feelings.

- What was I telling myself right before my mood changed?

  _____

  _____

  _____

- What does it mean to me when I feel _____ ? *(insert an emotion)*

  _____

  _____

  _____

- What am I afraid will happen in this situation? What do I predict will go wrong?

  _____

  _____

  _____

- When I feel _____ *(insert an emotion, such as scared)*, it means that I am _____ *(insert a noun or adjective, such as a weak person, incompetent, a failure)*.

  _____

  _____

  _____

Avoidance: The Behavior of Choice with Almost Anxiety

In response to his overwhelming thoughts and feelings, Jonathan had the desire to run away from his upcoming talks. Avoidance is the enemy when you're almost anxious. I consider it a behavior, even though it may seem like a *lack* of behavior. It's akin to the notion of an ostrich sticking its head into the ground.

Because there are nuances in how and why people engage in avoidance, I will spend more time helping you identify your avoidance patterns in the next chapter. But for now, I want to stress that avoidance was certainly an obstacle keeping Jonathan from building his own legacy by showing other teachers how to help troubled children.

To get unstuck from avoidant behavior, you must slow your mind. That's because by the time you notice a shift in your mood, you have likely moved on to other feelings. Usually that means you haven't even considered the thoughts that might be triggering your emotions. In fact, you might already have engaged in an avoidant behavior, like excusing yourself to go to the bathroom while in a meeting because you were feeling anxious.

As mindfulness meditation guru Jon Kabat-Zinn often says in his talks, our minds are like monkeys jumping from tree to tree, in constant motion. Most of the time, it's challenging just to slow your mind enough to pay attention to what is happening in there, let alone to try to separate the different aspects of the almost anxious wheel. Later in this book, we'll explore mindfulness skills to help you do this. But for now, I encourage you to bring a "beginner's mind" to this work and to treat these exercises as if this were the first time you've tried to do them, even if it's not. Being patient and having compassion toward yourself in this work will likely help you learn these skills much more easily.

Exercise 9.
Avoidance Wheel

Take a few minutes to think back to times when you managed your anxiety by avoiding a situation. For example, you might have let the phone go to voice mail, postponed a meeting, sought reassurance, or avoided panic and social-related triggers (such as a crowded movie theater.) Now list some of your own avoidant behaviors:

_____

_____

_____

_____

_____

Putting It All Together: General Principles for Developing Your Own Almost Anxious Wheel

You've learned how to individually examine your feelings, your thoughts, and your behaviors related to your almost anxious wheel. Now it's time to bring it all together in three steps and fill in a complete wheel.

Step 1: Decide Where to Start

One of the first questions my patients ask is, "Do I write down my thoughts first or my feelings? Is there a better place to start with my almost anxious wheel?" The answer is that there is no right or wrong way to draw your wheel. That's because the wheel turns in both directions. Whichever way the wheel gets going, once you are stuck on it, your thoughts, feelings, and behaviors feed off each other and keep the almost anxious cycle in motion.

As such, there are two good ways to begin: with your thoughts or your feelings/physical symptoms. If you're the type of person who pays more attention to your *feelings*, start there. Or if you are more centered in your head with your *thoughts*, it makes sense to list those first. The bottom line is that it doesn't matter where you begin, as long as you begin.

Step 2: Identify Your Thoughts and Feelings

Once you decide where to focus, you can then ask yourself, "How does _____ *(insert a thought)* make me feel? _____ *(insert an emotion)*." Alternatively, "What was I thinking about when I felt _____ *(insert an emotion or physical sensation)*?" Keep in mind that one thought might generate a *host* of emotions and vice versa. For example, if I had the thought "I am a lousy researcher" or "I will never be able to get through this workday," I might feel sad, scared, and over-whelmed. The more specific you are about your thoughts, emotions, and physical sensations, the better equipped you will be to apply the coping skills you'll read about in part 3 of this book.

Step 3: Identify Your Behavioral Response

When we feel strong, unpleasant emotions and physical sensations, we often want to avoid them. They're painful and distressing, so it's not surprising that the standard approach for many people is simply not to go there. However, there are many times when we cannot avoid them, so we try to get through them with white knuckles and clenched teeth. I certainly experienced that sensation as I became aware of my height phobia at Yosemite National Park.

For the sake of developing your own almost anxious wheel, ask yourself, "What do I do to manage unpleasant thoughts? What do I want to do to decrease these unpleasant feelings?" In other words, what is the behavior that you engage in to manage them? In Jonathan's case, he kept postponing the meeting with his boss to discuss plans to publicize his program.

Create Your Own Wheel

It's time to create your own wheel. Use the sample wheel in exercise 10 at the end of this chapter (or photocopy it or down-load it from www.AlmostAnxious.com; then you can use it for multiple situations). Begin by thinking of a recent fearful or worrisome event that you encountered. Then fill in your thoughts, feelings, and behaviors that resulted from the event.

Jonathan's Outcome

When he first came to see me, one of the first things Jonathan and I did together was develop his almost anxious wheel.

Then we moved on to other steps that I'll cover in the fol-lowing chapters:

- We tended to his basic needs of eating, sleeping, and exer-cising, which is necessary before tackling more nuanced cognitive and behavioral changes (chapter 7).

- When Jonathan felt slightly less depressed and more motivated, we targeted his thinking (chapter 9).

- Jonathan was able to arrive at more balanced thoughts and less rigid beliefs about the prospect of promoting his school curriculum. For example, he acknowledged that even though he might feel slightly anxious the first time he presented his curriculum to a large group of people, he knew his anxiety would decrease with time and he would be able to perform well.

- Despite his progress, he was still avoiding anything to do with planning the talks. So Jonathan and I "approached his lions" (chapter 10) and used several behavior techniques that helped him slowly and steadily approach his fear of public speaking.

- Through all of our work, Jonathan relied on his social support group (chapter 8), especially his wife and children, who continued to encourage him to approach his fears instead of avoiding them. They also helped him during times when he felt like giving up.

- To further help him face challenging situations, Jonathan learned a few mindfulness techniques (chapter 11).

I can't say this was a smooth ride for Jonathan. In fact, he would openly talk about how he felt like quitting many times through our work together. But he persevered, and with time, he developed the skills highlighted in this book and eventually overcame his almost anxiety. I haven't spoken with Jonathan in a while, but the last I heard, several school districts had implemented his curriculum, and he was "comfortably uncomfortable" giving presentations on how to implement his work. It remained slightly challenging for him, but he was approaching his fears instead of avoiding them.

• • •

By now, I hope you have identified your almost anxious subtype and feel capable of diagramming your own wheel. These skills will help you implement the skills that I'll describe in part 3 of this book. Each chapter in part 3 targets one or more of the areas on your almost anxious wheel (which you can find in exercise 10 and at www.AlmostAnxious.com).

Before we get there, you still need to put into place an important component of your foundation: tackling avoidance. This is a tricky topic, since avoidance often has positive short-term consequences that go along with its dreadful long-term ones. So, let's explore this enemy well in the next chapter; after all, only by learning all of the tactics of the enemy can you learn to overcome it.

Exercise 10.

My Own Almost Anxious Wheel

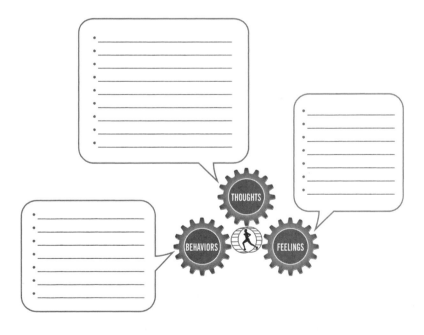

6

Anxiety or Avoidance
Focus on the True Enemy

When threatening situations strike, humans share other animals' natural tendency to fight or flee. But when almost anxiety is at play, another option arises: to avoid.

If I could have chosen a magical way to transport myself from the near top of Half Dome to the bottom of Yosemite Valley, and as a consequence avoid the high-altitude portion of my hike, I might have taken it. After all, I was momentarily paralyzed by the thought that I could fall at any point, stricken by my sudden realization that I was afraid of heights.

My natural inclination to choose avoidance under extreme anxiety is similar to the experience of my patients who are almost anxious. They face an "anxiety dilemma" and must decide between avoiding or approaching fear-provoking situations, each of which has short- and long-term consequences. I know I would have regretted it if I had not finished that hike, and I often hear the same refrain from my patients with almost anxiety. Leaving an anxiety-provoking situation because of fear often ends in regret, shame, and sadness.

Figure 12.
The "Approach versus Avoid" Dilemma

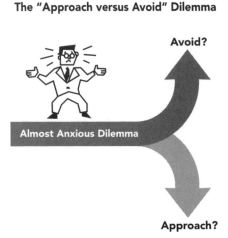

On its face, avoidance seems like it should be a fairly intuitive and easy concept to grasp. But avoidance is trickier to address than it first appears, and since it is the main reason people get stuck in the almost anxious wheel, it's worth exploring in depth.

Avoidance Can Appear in Many Disguises

Most of my patients come to me thinking they know *when* and *what* they are avoiding. For example, if you are afraid of heights and you skip the trip to the top of the Empire State Building during a family vacation to New York City, you are clearly avoiding a situation that makes you anxious. Overt avoidance behaviors like these are easy to identify.

But what about more subtle behaviors? Consider whether any of the following situations are also a form of avoidance:

- worrying about your vacation plans over and over, repeatedly wondering whether you will be able to get everything done before you leave

- asking your husband to reassure you that there is nothing wrong with you and that others are not making fun of you or thinking that you are dumb

- watching TV or listening to music as a form of distraction

- dragging a "wingman" (or "wingwoman") with you to a party where you don't know anyone to avoid facing the situation alone

- answering a question with another question because you are afraid that if you tell a stranger something about you, he or she will laugh at you

- engaging in safety behaviors, like carrying anxiety medication or a bottle of water with you in the subway in case you begin to have panic-like sensations in the enclosed space

So, are any of these examples types of avoidance? *Sometimes*!

To help you identify your avoidance, you first need to ask yourself, "What did I do to bring my anxiety down when _____ ?" *(Fill in the blank with your feared situation.)*

Simply put, you need to determine whether your behavioral response actually lowered your anxiety. Let's use my hiking example to illustrate what I mean. Here's the question I ask myself: "Why would I have considered turning around and hiking down the mountain instead of continuing the uphill hike?" There is only one answer: because I was afraid of falling! By turning around, I would have momentarily felt better, and my overall anxiety level would have decreased. As such, the consequence of my behavior would have been a decrease in my anxiety level, which I will call my anxiety temperature.

How about the almost anxious person who is afraid of social situations and brings along a "wingman" or "wingwoman" to a party? To determine whether this is a form of avoidance, this person must question whether having a companion reduces her overall anxiety level. If this person is afraid of public speaking but not particularly afraid to attend a party alone, then her anxiety might not change if she brings a friend with her. Accordingly, this behavior is probably not avoidance. In contrast, if she were to bring her friends to the next talk she is giving so that she feels less anxious, then her behavior probably is avoidance.

The bottom line is that *avoidance is anything you do that immediately brings your anxiety level down.*

Avoidance can involve taking action, but it also can be trying to not do an action when doing so would create discomfort. As such, avoidance does not have to be a clearly observable action. It could also be a thought or a subtle behavior, such as not making eye contact when asking someone out on a date. If your anxiety thermometer immediately decreases after your behavior, you are likely avoiding a situation.

Taking Your Anxiety Temperature

When treating people who have anxiety, many psychologists measure their patients' anxiety level using a scale called Subjective Units of Discomfort, or SUDs. I often tell my patients to think of their SUDs as their own internal anxiety thermometers, which are unique to them and calibrated to their individual anxiety levels.

As you think about avoidance, you can use the anxiety thermometer to help you gauge how anxious you become in situations and how much you would like to avoid those situations. You will likely find a direct relationship between your anxiety temperature and your desire to avoid a particular situation. The more anxious you get, the more likely you are to want to avoid it. As the anxiety thermometer in figure 13 illustrates, anxiety and avoidance range from 0 (no anxiety, no avoidance) to 100 (very severe anxiety, always avoid).

Here's something to keep in mind: people who are almost anxious can at times be perfectionists, wanting a perfect anxiety level. However, there is no perfect number in this case. After all, it is *your* own anxiety temperature.

Figure 13.
Anxiety/Avoidance Thermometer

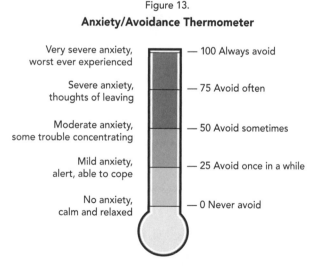

Very severe anxiety, worst ever experienced — 100 Always avoid

Severe anxiety, thoughts of leaving — 75 Avoid often

Moderate anxiety, some trouble concentrating — 50 Avoid sometimes

Mild anxiety, alert, able to cope — 25 Avoid once in a while

No anxiety, calm and relaxed — 0 Never avoid

Behaviors that lead to a *slow* decrease in anxiety do not constitute avoidance. In using this definition of "avoidance," I am talking about a sharp, fast drop in your anxiety temperature—like shifting from summer to winter, totally skipping fall!

To better understand avoidance, let's turn to my patient Katia's example.

Katia's Story

Katia is a well-groomed, soft-spoken mom who spent most of her life in the suburbs of Chicago. Shortly before seeing me, she had moved to Boston when her husband's workplace transferred him to the area. Not only was Katia adapting to a new city, but her youngest child had just left for college, and she was coping with empty-nest feelings.

The transition was hitting Katia hard, and her husband encouraged her to seek therapy. Although Katia was very poised in our first session, she looked tense, like a deer in headlights.

She said the concern that had led her to my office was her recent tendency to avoid things that she formerly enjoyed doing, which was beginning to restrict her life. In Chicago, she was able to balance her roles as wife and mother with her own identity. She was active in local charities and her children's school and athletic programs, and she had many friends at her gym, where she often took several spinning classes a week.

But since the move, she started to feel isolated and fearful. Katia's husband, Donald, urged her to volunteer through local nonprofits and at shelters, which were the types of activities that used to bring her great joy but now made her feel fearful.

As Katia's social isolation grew, so did her need to be around family. The only time she would feel calm was when her husband was home or after a phone call with her youngest child, Brie, who had moved to Los Angeles for college. Her family's reassurance that they were doing okay immediately relieved Katia's generalized worry. But as the months passed, these moments were becoming fewer and further between, with Donald busy at his new job and Brie focused on college. Yet they both sensed that if they didn't keep regular contact with Katia, she'd become more stressed and want even more time with them.

Her husband and daughter could only do so much to keep her calm. Katia told me that she had frustrated her entire family, but she didn't know how she could stop worrying if they didn't keep reassuring her that they were doing well. As we talked, it became clear that Katia was worrying about *many* things, not just her family's well-being. When pressed, she admitted that she wasn't really concerned about something bad happening to them—she needed to know that they would be there for her.

I was puzzled by Katia's self-imposed social restrictions. What had happened to her? Was she feeling a sadness that kept her from getting involved in her new community? Was she worried about how people on the East Coast would perceive her? After we talked for a while, I presented these theories to her and was surprised to find out that the central problem was something entirely different: Katia was afraid of driving.

Although she didn't like chaotic traffic around her, she had driven most of her life. To her, this meant that she "did not have any problems" driving. But in the past, Katia had orchestrated her life in a way that protected her from really having to face her driving fears. For example, she lived in a quiet suburban area without major traffic. And she tried to avoid driving at night whenever possible. When I asked what she was afraid might happen while she was driving, Katia said that when she was just learning how to drive at sixteen, she'd had a panic attack. This had really scared her, and she had tried to stop

107

driving, afraid that something was physically wrong with her or that she might have another panic attack while driving. But her mother was a very busy woman who didn't have time to drive her around. She pushed Katia to get her driver's license until she finally did so at age seventeen.

Katia may have been at the threshold for a diagnosis of panic disorder when the attack first happened. Katia was terrified of the possibility that while driving she could lose control because of a panic attack and injure someone else. Because her mother encouraged her to continue approaching her fears and not give in to the fear of another attack, she likely overcame most of it. Nonetheless, she started to use *subtle* forms of avoidance. She limited her driving to necessary times and ensured that, whenever possible, she had a safety person with her—someone who could help her if she had a panic attack. In high school, she would always invite her best friend and neighbor, Suzanne, to come along when she had to drive. "Having Suzanne there just made me feel more comfortable, and she liked getting out of her house," she said.

The move to Boston plunged her into a large, fast-moving city. Boston is notorious for its narrow alleys (which used to be horse and buggy paths), aggressive drivers, and poorly marked streets (there was once a *Saturday Night Live* sketch in which game show contestants had to navigate the city relying on Dunkin' Donuts locations!).

To make matters worse, Katia's daughter was no longer available to ride with her. *That* is the factor that was both keeping her at home and fueling her need to call her daughter. She had driven into the city a few times but didn't like doing it, even when it wasn't rush hour. "If I commit to anything, people might expect me to drive into Boston," she explained. "My husband is at work and I don't know many people. What if I can't find someone to drive into the city with me? I might not be able to do it, and that means I would let people down."

By the time I started to work with Katia, she was very close to a clinical diagnosis of panic disorder. But since she hadn't given up driving entirely (she could still do it, although with white knuckles wrapped tightly around the wheel) and was only reporting moderate distress, she was still within the almost anxious range.

We set to work on shifting her thoughts and behaviors related to driving, which meant addressing her avoidance.

Shades of Avoidance

The first step in designing a treatment plan for Katia was to delve into her avoidance. Like many of my patients, Katia had originally believed that avoidance was either a yes-or-no, black-or-white concept; either you avoided or you didn't. Yet, when you view avoidance as anything that quickly brings your anxiety thermometer down, you can see a gradient to avoidance, with shades ranging from more overt behaviors, such as refusing to drive into Boston, to more subtle behaviors, like asking for reassurance from her family.

Katia was puzzled at my excitement over trying to discover the entire spectrum of her avoidance behaviors. Unlike me, she was not feeling thrilled. From her perspective, these behaviors had been ingrained in her life for a while, and they were a symbol of how distressed she was feeling when we met. I, however, am usually happy when people are able to identify their whole range of avoidance strategies. If avoidance is your enemy, you have to know your enemy well to win the war!

Here's a fuller look at the many shades of avoidance. Do you recognize any from your own life?

Behavioral Avoidance

I've found that most people think avoidance is solely a behavior that they *didn't* do because of fear. For example, if you're afraid of dogs, you might not visit your best friend's home because she has two pit bulls—or even a poodle. You might also go jogging but only on streets without parks, to cut down on the chance of encountering an unleashed dog.

This is an *overt*, or obvious, type of avoidance, and it's indeed one of the classic forms of avoidance among the various anxiety disorders and types of almost anxiety.

Please read through the following checklists and check any behaviors that you use in your own life to bring your anxiety temperature down. You can also download exercise 11 at www .AlmostAnxious.com.

Exercise 11.
Overt Types of Avoidance Checklist

I find myself avoiding the following *social situations* because I'm afraid that

- I might do or say something that would embarrass or humiliate me.
- others will think I am weird or strange.
- others will make fun of me.

Social Situations

- ☐ Giving presentations
- ☐ Being an active participant in small groups (like in business meetings or at school)

☐ Talking to strangers, either in person or on the phone

☐ Social events (such as parties, sporting events, dance clubs)

☐ Asking someone out on a date

☐ Other: _____

I find myself avoiding the following *everyday situations* because I'm afraid that

- I might develop panic-like symptoms.
- if I were to have panic-like symptoms, I might lose control or embarrass myself.
- if I were to have panic-like symptoms, I might not be able to get help.

Everyday Situations

☐ Public transportation (subway, bus, airplane, train)

☐ Small enclosed places (such as elevators or small rooms)

☐ Activities that increase my heart rate (like exercise, sex, going up the stairs, dancing)

☐ Drinking coffee or other stimulating substances

☐ Driving, because it might induce panic-like symptoms

☐ Other: _____

I sometimes use these other avoidance behaviors:

_____

_____

_____

_____

_____

Subtle Avoidance

Although at times you might be able to completely avoid something that makes you fearful, when you're still in the almost anxious territory, you are likely to also have more subtle types of avoidance behaviors.

My definition for subtle avoidance is *when you find a way to mold an activity or experience so you can engage in it with less anxiety*. In essence, you are doing something to try to bring your anxiety down to a level at which you can actually participate. In the psychology literature, subtle avoidance attempts are often considered "safety behaviors." For people with social anxiety, common safety behaviors include avoiding eye contact and mentally rehearsing what you'll say before speaking. Individuals with panic disorder also frequently use safety behaviors like holding on to a support person to avoid fainting or falling.[1]

Take a few minutes to reflect on your own feared or worrisome experiences and consider whether you engaged in any of the following activities in an attempt to decrease your anxiety temperature. Work through the checklist in exercise 12, which can also be downloaded at www.AlmostAnxious.com.

Exercise 12.
Subtle Types of Avoidance Checklist

Check any of the following activities you do in an effort to reduce your anxiety:

☐ Bringing anxiety medication, even if you don't currently use it, everywhere you go, in case you have a panic attack

☐ Sitting in the aisle seat on the plane so you can get up if you start experiencing panic symptoms

☐ Not making eye contact while talking with others

☐ Answering a question with a question to avoid having to talk more

☐ Keeping to yourself at parties

☐ Avoiding shaking hands, so others don't notice your sweaty palms

☐ Talking softly

☐ Keeping your hands in your pockets to avoid showing jitteriness

☐ Wearing light summer clothes in the winter to help prevent nervous sweating

I sometimes use these other safety behaviors or subtle forms of avoidance:

_____

_____

_____

When Seeking Reassurance Becomes Avoidance

Whenever you feel stressed or worried, it's nice to be able to reach out to someone who can reassure you that you'll be able to handle whatever situation you are worried about. However, reassurance seeking can function as a form of avoidance, since it immediately reduces your anxiety level. It can also get you stuck on your almost anxious "hamster wheel" by keeping you from facing your fears.

Be very mindful that you don't cross the line into avoidance when you ask someone to provide you with reassurance. Here are some signs that the reassurance you seek is becoming an avoidance strategy:

- The relief you sense when someone reassures you is short-lived, and you feel compelled to ask for reassurance about the same topic over and over.
- You find yourself rearranging your questions to get reassurance again.
- The *only* way you can manage your almost anxiety is by checking in with someone about the specific fear.

Whenever my patients become concerned that they're seeking reassurance too often, I suggest that they make a "contract" with their friends and loved ones. This agreement specifies that they're allowed to seek reassurance only *once* per topic. If they start to ask the same question over and over again, the other party has the right to point out what's happening.

When Katia asked her friend or daughter to come with her on drives, she was using subtle avoidance. This does help the person engage in the worrisome or feared activity with less anxiety. Yet people can become a prisoner of the avoidance itself, limiting their engagement in the activity to times when their "security blanket" is present (and it might not always be).

The Short- and Long-term Consequences of Avoidance

Avoidance has temporary *positive* results, which is one reason that most of my patients who are almost anxious get stuck in it. When you engage in avoidance, it gives you a momentary sense of relief, which your brain quickly interprets as "avoidance helps me to feel better."

The story of one of my patients, Mike, provides a good example of the short-term benefits of avoidance.

Mike's Story

Mike was an African American IT analyst in his late thirties who worked at a large hospital in Boston.

He had always been mildly anxious in social situations, which is one of the reasons he had gone into the IT field—it didn't require him to interact with a lot of other people. Mike described himself as mildly anxious but happy overall. However, one situation consistently triggered his fears: parties!

Mike would start to worry about parties weeks in advance. "Will I know anyone there? Will people notice that I am shy? Will I be able to have a good time?" he would ask himself. As you can imagine, these anticipatory worries would usually raise Mike's anxiety temperature slightly.

However, one party in particular always made him extra anxious: his parents' annual family get-together. Mike disliked having to answer personal questions from nosy relatives at these events. But he was close to his family and felt it was impossible for him to avoid the party, so he had found subtle ways to "white knuckle" through the experience by using subtle avoidance.

Figure 14 shows what happened to Mike's anxiety temperature during last year's party.

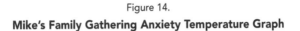

Figure 14.
Mike's Family Gathering Anxiety Temperature Graph

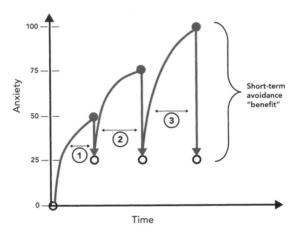

As Mike walked into the party, his anxiety temperature started to increase (phase 1). The first person he bumped into was his cousin Peter, who had just married a Mexican woman who spoke little English. She was very outgoing and friendly and wanted to talk to Mike.

Mike's immediate thoughts were, "I won't be able to understand her. She will think that I am rude. My cousin will be mad that I didn't attend their wedding." As Mike started to talk to the couple, his anxiety temperature continued to increase, reaching a peak of 50. He was starting to feel uncomfortable and slightly warm. So he took steps to avoid the situation.

Avoidance: Mike excused himself from the conversation, saying that he had just arrived and was feeling thirsty, so he was going to grab a beer.

Short-term consequence: By walking away, Mike immediately felt better and his anxiety temperature went down.

Beer in hand, Mike noticed his dad walking toward him. His mind began racing again: "Will he ask me if I am saving money to buy a house? Will he ask if I am going to step up and try to become a manager in my department?" (phase 2). This time, Mike started to get more of the physical sensations of anxiety, feeling even hotter and now slightly light-headed. By the time he was actually talking to his dad, Mike's anxiety temperature had reached a 75 on his thermometer. He again took evasive action.

Avoidance: Mike told his father that he urgently needed to go to the bathroom but they could continue their conversation later.

Short-term consequence: Mike walked upstairs so he could have time away from people. This made him feel much better as his anxiety temperature dropped again.

Walking downstairs to rejoin the party a few minutes later, Mike spotted his aunt Isabel, a gregarious housewife and mother of five, who Mike knew was well intentioned and loved him very much. But he also knew that she prided herself on knowing other people's business. His thoughts raced again. "Will she ask if I am dating someone? Will she remind me that I am getting close to forty and my time for having children is growing short?"

This time, Mike's anxiety went through the roof. He immediately began to tremble and feel dizzy, hot, and very anxious (phase 3). Mike used yet another avoidance tactic.

Avoidance: He turned around and went back upstairs to his parents' bedroom, shut the door, and turned on the TV. This distracted him and kept him from having to speak with his aunt.

Short-term consequence: As Mike started to watch a football game, he felt relief. But this time, something else started to happen. Mike also began to feel sad and disappointed with himself. He knew his aunt just wanted a friendly conversation, and he had avoided her. He wondered about the other emotional consequences of his avoiding others. Was this what his life would be like forever, with one avoidance episode after another?

• • •

Because avoidance provides a momentary sense of relief, it's self-reinforcing. It feels good, so people keep turning to it.

Yet this self-reinforcing quick fix also robs people of the chance to learn what would happen if they repeatedly engaged in the situation that worries them. In this way, it actually *prolongs* anxiety problems and worry.[2] In other words, despite the short-term benefits, avoidance produces problematic long-term consequences.

Going back to Katia's story, she felt an immediate reprieve from her worry when she spoke to her husband or daughter in the car, distracted herself with a Bruce Springsteen CD, or reserved her driving obligations to non-rush-hour time. At these moments, Katia felt better and didn't have to face her anxiety.

But what were the long-term consequences of Katia's avoidance? Although I can't be 100 percent certain, it is likely that if Katia would have continued in her avoidance pattern, her life would have become even more isolated—reducing her chance to make new friends and engage in hobbies and reducing her sense of purpose in life. Fast-forwarding months and years, it is likely that Katia's continuous reassurance seeking might have further upset her husband, which in turn could lead to marital problems.

For most people with anxiety problems, it's not the anxiety itself that prevents them from engaging in the situation (even though that is what most of my patients believe). Instead, it's their *interpretation* of what will happen if they face the situation. For example, individuals with social anxiety tend to avoid situations where they believe they will be judged or evaluated negatively.

However, if you never face your fears, you don't get to learn that your worst predicted outcome usually doesn't transpire, *and that even if it were to come true, you could actually survive it.* This is an important experience that people who are almost anxious need to have.

I have tried to explain this concept to patients for a decade, and the most helpful example I use is from a colleague and friend of mine, Fátima, who truly experienced what some would consider the "worst-case scenario."

Fátima's Story

Just three weeks after she delivered her second baby, Fátima was scheduled to discuss her research in front of five hundred people. Being a dedicated professional, she fought through her sleep deprivation and went to give the talk. While sitting on stage as part of a panel, she noticed that she was feeling queasy. She asked herself, "Why do I feel this way? Did I not sleep enough? Did I pick up the stomach bug that my three-year-old daughter has? Is there a chance that I'm about to throw up in front of this audience?" As you can imagine, these thoughts just got her more wound up. Before it was her turn to talk, she rushed off stage and made it to the restroom, where she did indeed get sick.

This brought her a lot of attention, though not the type she wanted. A conference organizer followed her into the bathroom and asked if she needed help. Someone had to call her husband to pick her up. She wasn't able to give her talk. All in all, this was close to being a worst-case scenario (although at least she got off stage first!).

However, Fátima survived the situation with her reputation intact. She had predicted that the organization hosting the conference would be upset with her and not invite her back, and that her academic career might be tainted by this episode. However, the complete opposite happened! Over the next few days, she received many emails from colleagues checking in to ensure that she was okay and to offer help if she needed anything.

· · ·

My friend shared her story with me so I could use it to remind people with anxiety—and almost anxiety—that even if the worst-case outcome you fear *does* happen, you can tolerate it.

This would turn out to be an important lesson for Katia. And I was happy about that, since research has found a relationship between avoidance and psychological problems. For example, avoidance behavior among individuals with social anxiety can lead to depression.[3] This isn't surprising, given that anxiety and depression often go hand in hand. I tell my patients, "When you are thinking about avoiding something, remember that you may be choosing between feeling anxious or feeling depressed, but neither will make your life better."

Like anxiety, depression tends to limit people's engagement in life and can stop them from taking part in activities they used to enjoy because they feel too sad or blue. But this in turn can further increase their depression.[4] They may then find themselves in a self-fulfilling cycle of depression that leads to avoidance, which then increases their long-term anxiety and generates even more depression.

Avoidance has also been linked to substance abuse in people with panic symptoms. Specifically, people who are fearful of having panic-like symptoms might drink in an effort to suppress some of the sensations related to the panic.[5] Yet, given the physical effects of alcohol use and abuse (including hangovers), people often find themselves feeling *more* anxious after drinking, instead of less anxious.

Consider the short-term benefits and long-term costs of avoidance by working through exercise 13. You can also download this exercise at www.AlmostAnxious.com.

Exercise 13.
Short-Term Benefits and Long-Term Costs of Avoidance

Read through the list of short-term benefits and long-term consequences of avoidance. Are the benefits worth enduring the negative consequences? Add your own short-term benefits and long-term consequences to the lists.

SHORT-TERM BENEFITS OF AVOIDANCE	LONG-TERM CONSEQUENCES OF AVOIDANCE
❏ Immediate decrease in anxiety temperature	❏ Get forever stuck on the "Hamster Wheel"
• _____	❏ Social isolation
• _____	❏ Depression
• _____	❏ Alcoholism
• _____	❏ Marital/relational problems
• _____	❏ Increased anxiety
• _____	❏ Occupational problems
• _____	❏ Loneliness
• _____	❏ Family conflict
• _____	• _____
• _____	• _____
• _____	• _____

Katia's Outcome

Katia spent a lot of time getting close to her avoidance enemy. She created a list of her avoidance patterns and also wrote down the short-term benefits and long-term consequences of her avoidance.

In this process, Katia and I worked on broadening her thinking and challenging her belief that the worst-case scenario would happen whenever she drove alone.

Next, Katia worked on facing her avoidance behaviors by actively engaging in situations that would induce panic-like sensations. She would push herself to stay in the situation until her anxiety temperature went down. She repeated this process (called exposure therapy) over and over again, until she learned that (1) the worst-case scenario indeed did not happen and (2) as she approached her anxiety, it naturally came down slowly. Later in this book, we'll discuss how you, too, can develop these skills.

• • •

As Katia learned, anxiety is upsetting. It signals danger! But it is not the enemy. The enemy is avoidance. Remember that avoidance is sneaky: it often slips into your life unnoticed, it keeps itself going by providing you temporary relief, and over the long term it limits your quality of life and makes you a prisoner of your own mind.

It's time now to shift to the third section of the book, which offers you an anxiety-reducing tool kit. The next chapters will teach you how to capitalize on your almost anxiety so it helps you instead of hindering your life!

Part 3

Your Anxiety Tool Kit

7

Let's Get Physical!

When you're exploring how you may have used techniques like avoidance to manage your anxiety in the past, you may focus on psychological factors and overlook physical factors that could be at play. Jenny's case is a good example.

Jenny's Story

When I met her, Jenny had recently graduated from a prestigious college. At twenty-five, she was the first from her large family of Chinese immigrants to go to college. She felt obligated to do well academically, because her parents had each worked two jobs to pay for her education.

She made excellent grades, became her class salutatorian, and landed a good job right after graduation. But her drive to excel came at a price. She didn't date much in college, though she told me this didn't really bother her. At first, it seemed that Jenny was seeking help with changing her behaviors, in particular anything related to her weight gain, poor sleep, and diet, which she thought were the reasons she was feeling depressed lately.

But as our conversation continued, it became clear that Jenny had a rising level of anxiety, which she said was growing out of control. She was struggling with poor concentration and constantly felt tired. Thus, although her weight and diet had brought her to my office, she really needed help with her anxiety, which was contributing to her other concerns.

Jenny told me that her family had a history of anxiety, but they usually didn't talk about it. She knew that her mom took medication for this problem, but culturally it was not appropriate for them to discuss mental health issues. So Jenny felt that she needed to keep her anxiety a secret from those around her. In fact, throughout college Jenny never told anyone that she was feeling increasingly anxious.

Most of the factors that triggered her anxiety were related to performance, either social or academic. She was concerned that people would think less of her because of her Chinese accent, so she tried to speak English as perfectly as possible and overprepared for presentations. Despite these fears, Jenny didn't turn away from the things that made her anxious. As a result, her performance-related fears would not have been significant enough for a clinician to diagnose her with social anxiety disorder. Yet here Jenny was in my office, telling me about this anxiety that was limiting her ability to fully enjoy life.

I was intrigued by how Jenny managed to keep her anxiety contained enough to be successful in college and her workplace. I also wondered why her anxiety had gotten significantly worse after graduating. When I asked her these questions, Jenny's face grew bright red and she looked down at the floor.

"Don't you see?" she said. "I just eat my feelings. Every time I am anxious, I go for a cookie, french fries, or something that makes me feel better immediately. I don't stuff myself, but I make sure I have snacks around so I can 'manage' my anxiety. Eating helps immediately with my anxiety, but now that I'm getting overweight, I know I need to do something else."

Jenny's relationship with food changed when she was a freshman in college, which is not unusual. She had always lived with her family, who ensured that she ate balanced meals, got enough sleep, and followed a healthy exercise routine. Her dad was a firm believer in Eastern philosophy and had taught Jenny how to do tai chi and practice mindfulness. In retrospect, as Jenny pondered her anxiety elevation in college, she speculated that her parents' close attention to her physical and emotional needs might have served to keep her anxiety at bay when she was younger.

But this careful tending went out the window her first week of college. The stress of pursuing high grades, making new friends, and adjusting to college life—combined with the lack of structure—all culminated in new imbalances. Jenny started to eat more, sleep less, drink coffee, and abandon her exercise routine. She didn't give much thought to the resulting lack of energy, figuring it was due to her singular focus on making good grades.

By the time she came home during her first winter break, her body's internal clock was completely unregulated: she lacked a regular schedule for even basic routines, such as eating and sleeping. At that time, she had only put on a few pounds. More notable to her parents was that she was acting a little more anxious, sleeping odd hours, and eating fattier foods in larger amounts. Yet, they didn't recommend that she adjust these new patterns.

Jenny's experience her first semester of college is not that different from a lot of freshmen's. After all, this is a period that challenges young people's preexisting patterns, which are often set in place by their parents and family routines. (This is an important reminder to all of us: changes make it harder to stick to our routines.) As such, Jenny was probably right not to be concerned right away. However, she had a family history of anxiety, and her underlying predisposition combined with her behavioral changes in college were contributing to her panicky feelings.

Jenny said her anxiety was like a hollow feeling in the pit of her stomach, almost like she was hungry. That's why she started to eat when she was anxious, even though she eventually realized that she wasn't really hungry.

Because she was so preoccupied with her grades, she often stayed up late to study, sometimes getting as little as four hours of sleep a night. So she felt like she deserved a treat when her roommates suggested ordering late-night pizza and breadsticks. She'd been working hard, hadn't she? She then started to manage her morning sleepiness with big breakfasts (she loved bacon, egg, and cheese sandwiches) and coffee, which she sipped throughout the day. The coffee jitters, in turn, ended up affecting her ability to sleep the next night.

And thus, her vicious cycle started. Eating more led to feelings of sluggishness. The lack of energy led to less exercise. These both affected her ability to sleep, which was also affected by her caffeine intake. So it wasn't a big surprise to me that by the end of college, not only was Jenny's anxiety inflated, but she was also having a lot of trouble sleeping, which interfered with her ability to concentrate.

During college, she could have an erratic schedule, but that was not possible in her new nine-to-five job as a marketing professional. Additionally, her job made it difficult to use food as a coping strategy. She couldn't just leave a meeting to get a cookie if she was anxious, so she often was unable to manage her anxiety. And her fatigue and work schedule left her with little energy or time to return to her teenage exercise routine.

Although it was likely that Jenny and I would need to work on other factors that contributed to her anxiety, such as her thought patterns, I was certain that we first needed to help her regulate her "engine." Jenny's college experience was akin to driving a car for four years on low-quality gasoline and skipping service checkups and oil changes. With such inattention, it is not surprising that Jenny's engine was running poorly and that her attempts to treat her feelings with junk food and coffee were making her motor run more erratically. It was time for a maintenance checkup!

Busy Lives Pull People Away from the Basics

In my work as a researcher, clinical psychologist, and writer, there are times when I feel stretched so thin that I wonder how *anything* will get done. In a typical week, I must supervise students, meet deadlines for grants, see patients, write papers, and plan conferences. In short, my hours are stuffed with the same types of obligations that make modern life so hectic for many people.

You, too, will always have multiple demands competing for the same pool of time:

- your personal needs, including your roles as a family member (mother, father, daughter, son, and so on)
- work needs (scheduled work hours, late nights and weekends on special projects)
- social needs (activities with friends and family)
- physiological needs (eating, sleep, and exercise)

Unfortunately, the first needs that usually go unanswered when people are stressed are the activities that actually keep almost anxiety at bay. These needs include proper nutrition, relaxation, and exercise. Researchers have found that people who are asked to complete a stressful task are more likely to snack on unhealthy foods (like candy or chips) than healthy foods (like fruit or nuts), as compared with people who are asked to complete a nonstressful task. Research also confirms that greater stress is associated with a greater drive to eat, including binge eating.[1]

In addition, plenty of research suggests that anxiety and stress are associated with poor sleep quality or insomnia and a sedentary lifestyle.[2] If you neglect any of these needs, you are more likely to become almost anxious (or gain a full-blown anxiety disorder). My own clinical practice experience parallels the scientific data. Several of my patients have trouble differentiating their anxiety from their hunger or fatigue.

The problem with these stress-induced unhealthy behaviors is that they keep you stuck on the almost anxious wheel. What puzzles me the most about this is that people somehow find a way to manage to meet their *other* obligations because they consider them a "must." For example, when was the last time that you missed the Super Bowl or a movie that you were excited to see, forgot to pick up your kids from day care, or blew off an important meeting with your company's CEO? When have you missed a session at the gym because you were on deadline?

People manage to prioritize their schedules enough to get *certain* things done. So why is it that so many people don't put their physical health into the equation? Why is it that so many take better care of their cars than their own bodies and minds?

Nowadays, cars are so "smart" that they even tell you what they need. Most cars have a warning signal that lights up, for example, when the oil needs to be changed or the tire pressure is low. Engineers put these alerts in place to tell you when it is time to attend to your car's needs so you're not left stranded alongside the road.

In some ways, our needs as humans—eating, sleeping, and exercising—are analogous to the needs of our cars. Your mind can perform nimbly, hopping from task to task and zooming from zero to sixty in an instant. Your car may also handle like a dream, zipping around curves and responding with a burst of speed the moment you need it. But if *any* of your car's basic needs is left unmet—a leaky tire, a dead battery, or an empty gas tank—you're not going to enjoy its fine-tuned driving abilities. Likewise, if you ignore any of *your* basic needs, you're not going to be able to race between your obligations with your mind shifting gears smoothly while you operate at peak concentration and just the right level of anxiety.

In this chapter, I will discuss the three most important bodily needs—good nutrition, sleep, and exercise—that you *must* address before you can bring your almost anxiety down to an optimal level. I know that people have been telling you since grade school that you need to eat better, go to sleep earlier, and exercise more. (These steps are seemingly prescribed as the solution for most of our mental and physical health woes!) But they truly are the foundation for taming almost anxiety. Plenty of studies point to a back-and-forth relationship between anxiety and eating, sleeping, and exercise. For example, researchers found that high anxiety predicts the onset of insomnia, and insomnia predicts future episodes of anxiety.[3] I see this relationship in my own office. Patients who are sleep deprived often complain of heightened anxiety. Conversely, patients who are under a lot of stress are more likely to have sleeping problems.

The good news is that making healthy lifestyle choices can help reduce your anxiety. As such, it's time to repair each one of these issues before learning more advanced skills to decrease your almost anxiety.

Fueling Your Gas Tank: The Role of Food in Managing Almost Anxiety

As I observed with Jenny, sometimes people have trouble knowing whether they're anxious or hungry. This is especially true for those who have lived with moderate levels of anxiety for a while. As soon as some of my patients start to feel a little anxious, they do one of two things:

- They reach for a cookie, candy bar, or bag of chips.
- Or they end up at the other end of the spectrum and completely avoid food, skipping meals or even fasting.

Research suggests that about 36 percent of people eat more than usual when they feel stressed and another 26 percent restrict their eating when they feel stressed.[4]

Either of these behaviors serves as an avoidance technique. One of the main premises of this book is that *anxiety itself is not the enemy.* Instead, it's avoidance, broadly defined as an effort you take to bring your anxiety down immediately, that maintains your almost anxious feelings. This avoidance is what you should be targeting. As such, using food as a way to avoid your anxiety will only produce one outcome: more anxiety. So what should you do instead?

For starters, if you are a healthy adult, aim to keep your overall glucose (blood sugar) level at a steady range.[5] When you eat a carbohydrate-rich food (like a candy bar or baked snack), your body quickly breaks it down into sugar. When this sugar hits your bloodstream, your pancreas produces a rush of the hormone insulin to help your body's cells take in the sugar. As a result, your blood sugar can quickly rise, then fall.

Research suggests that changes in your glucose level—the amount of sugar in your bloodstream—can lead to hypoglycemia (low blood sugar), which can lead to negative mood states like irritability and anger.[6] Low glucose has also been shown to hinder your ability to handle cognitive tasks, and it's likely to interfere in your concentration as well.[7]

This research supports the notion that before trying to change your anxiety with psychological approaches, it is very important to manage your food intake. That means paying close attention to *how often* you are eating and *what* you are eating.

I suggest to most of my patients that they begin keeping a simple record of their diet and mood to get a sense of how the two are related. If you know that your eating habits have a negative impact on your sense of well-being, because you're eating either too much or not enough, I would recommend that you keep tabs on yourself using the form in exercise 14

Exercise 14.
My Food and Anxiety Log

DATE / DAY	BREAKFAST			LUNCH			DINNER			SNACK
	Anxiety Before (0-100)	Food (Yes/No)	Anxiety After (0-100)	Anxiety Before (0-100)	Food (Yes/No)	Anxiety After (0-100)	Anxiety Before (0-100)	Food (Yes/No)	Anxiety After (0-100)	(Yes/No)
/ Monday										
/ Tuesday										
/ Wednesday										
/ Thursday										
/ Friday										
/ Saturday										
/ Sunday										

(you can download it from www.AlmostAnxious.com). For the next week, write down how you feel from 0 (no anxiety) to 100 (the most anxiety you've ever felt) before and after you eat something. You don't have to change what you are eating or go on a diet. Just track the food in broad categories, along with a score for your mood.

After keeping track of your diet and mood with this form for a week, you may want to consider making some changes in your eating habits to promote a lower level of anxiety.

• • •

In the course of any given year, you're likely to encounter dozens, perhaps hundreds, of recommendations for what foods you should and shouldn't eat. Many dietary guidelines are con- troversial, and they tend to change with time. I am not going to wade deeply into any food debates. Instead, I want to focus on research-supported advice that has helped many of my patients find a more balanced level of anxiety:

- **Always eat breakfast:** Research indicates that people who eat breakfast are less likely to be obese (which can be a source of anxiety). Habitually skipping breakfast has also been linked to a variety of health concerns that can also encourage anxiety.[8] Most of my patients who are almost anxious are more likely to feel anxious when they are hungry. This makes a lot of sense, since skipping a meal can lead to temporary hypoglycemia, which might mimic anxiety symptoms. If you start your day with some food in your stomach, you are more likely to continue eating at a regular pace during the following hours, which might prevent hunger that you interpret as anxiety.

- **Eat on a regular schedule:** To keep your blood sugar steady, it's important to eat frequently. Some of my patients find that eating small meals more often helps them stay recharged for longer periods compared to eating only two or three large meals in a day. In general, I suggest that you start by eating three small meals and three snacks spread throughout the day. Monitor how that affects your concentration, energy level, and almost anxiety.

- **Eat wholesome foods:** Diets rich in essential vitamins and minerals, such as B vitamins and iron, are important for the healthy function of neurotransmitters: those important mood-affecting brain chemicals such as serotonin, dopamine, norepinephrine, and GABA. Research suggests that healthy functioning of these brain chemicals, and therefore our moods, may be affected by our vitamin intake. Experts recommend eating a "rainbow diet" rich in fruits and vegetables of various colors.[9]

- **Monitor your alcohol intake:** Alcohol use is associated with depression, and alcohol at high doses indirectly affects anxiety by disturbing sleep.[10] The National Institute on Alcohol Abuse and Alcoholism recommends that you (1) limit alcohol to no more than four drinks per day for men and three for women, (2) have no more than fourteen drinks per week for men and seven for women, and (3) pace yourself while drinking so you don't take in too much alcohol too quickly.

Jenny was unusual among her college friends in that she didn't use alcohol to manage her almost anxiety. Laurel, her roommate, also had excessive anxiety, but instead of going for the cookie jar, Laurel would reach into the fridge for beers on nights that she was particularly anxious. Jenny noticed, however, that Laurel was always more anxious on the days after she drank.

For that reason, Jenny avoided drinking, since she was afraid it would make her more anxious over the long term. And she was correct! Plenty of evidence suggests that alcohol is associated with more anxiety. Researchers have learned that alcohol use and anxiety symptoms reinforce one another in a destructive, self-perpetuating cycle.[11]

When Laurel drank, she would fall asleep faster, but she didn't sleep as restfully as she did on nights when she didn't drink. Lack of sleep not only inhibits your concentration; it also makes you more anxious. As with eating, I would suggest that you monitor your alcohol intake, and if you notice the patterns I just described, cut back on your drinking.

How Do I Change My Eating Habits?

These steps for healthier eating have helped many of my patients:

- Always make sure your pantry, refrigerator, and cupboards are well stocked with a variety of nutritious foods.
- Carry a healthy snack with you.
- Don't wait until you arc hungry to cat. Eating small meals and snacks throughout the day helps keep your glucose level steady, which lessens your almost anxiety.

- Find a support person (or people) to help you. If you are trying to change *any* of your habits, having someone you can call on for encouragement and understanding helps. This is especially true when you are changing your eating habits, as you are likely to often eat with other people. Let your support team know about the changes you're trying to make, and ask for their help.

Sleep: The "Overnight" Method for Dealing with Almost Anxiety

Jenny's struggles with getting good sleep weren't unusual. In an evolutionary sense, anxiety increases people's alertness so they can respond to threats by fighting or fleeing. As a result, even when you're merely almost anxious, you are going to be more alert and, as many of my patients report, more jittery. Once Jenny found herself stuck in the almost anxious wheel, her thoughts would keep her awake. She would start to worry about work the next day, constantly check the clock, and have trouble falling asleep, which made waking up more difficult the next morning.

Similar to Jenny, my patient Samantha, an in-demand neurosurgeon, often commented during our sessions that she felt as though her anxiety propelled her during her busy days, but it hindered her at home. Her mind was always racing and she never felt present in the moment, which also kept her up at night.

According to research, being sleep deprived can raise your anxiety level significantly, and vice versa. Researchers have found that people who have been diagnosed with anxiety disorder have an increased risk for insomnia and shorter sleep duration.[12]

Given the back-and-forth association between sleep and anxiety, taking stock of your sleep patterns can help you figure out whether you need to adjust your sleep schedule as a step in addressing your anxiety. To assess your sleep habits using exercise 15, fill in the sleep log for a week; you can also download this log at www.AlmostAnxious.com.

If you are consistently sleeping fewer than six hours a night, if you have trouble falling asleep or staying asleep, or if you wake up feeling tired or sluggish, chances are good that you would benefit from better sleep. Practice the following sleep guidelines for at least two weeks while you keep tabs on your almost anxiety symptoms.

Dos and Don'ts for Better Sleep

Dos

- Practice relaxing exercises, such as stretching or calming yoga.
- Use your bed for sleep and sex only.
- Engage in relaxing activities before going to bed, such as taking a warm bath, reading a novel, or meditating.
- Eat a small snack before bed—being hungry can interfere with sleep.
- Get out of bed if you can't fall asleep after twenty minutes; then practice relaxing activities.
- Maintain a regular sleep cycle, with consistent sleep and wake time.
- If you wake up in the middle of the night for fifteen minutes or more, get out of bed.
- Keep a comfortable temperature in your bedroom.

Exercise 15.
My Sleep Log

DATE / DAY	Trouble Falling Asleep (Yes/No)	Difficulty Staying Asleep (Yes/No)	Waking Up Earlier Than Desired (Yes/No)	Waking Up Rested (Yes/No)	Total Hours of Sleep (# Hrs.)
/ Monday					
/ Tuesday					
/ Wednesday					
/ Thursday					
/ Friday					
/ Saturday					
/ Sunday					

Don'ts

- Use stimulating devices (such as a computer, TV, or iPad) before bed.

- Drink alcohol close to bed time.

- Stare at a clock—this is guaranteed to keep you up worrying.

- Exercise vigorously before bed.

- Smoke close to bed time—nicotine is stimulating.

- Drink coffee or eat chocolate right before bed— caffeine is stimulating.

- Have disrupting light and noise around while in bed.

- Take worries to bed.

Research also suggests that a brief nap (approximately thirty minutes or less) can improve alertness and reduce sleepiness during the day, without disrupting sleep that night.[13] If you are feeling sleepy or sluggish during the day, you might find a short nap to be helpful.

Use Exercise to Keep Your Battery Charged

One of the biggest lifestyle myths that people fall for is that one must *have* energy to *expend* energy in exercise. (People hint at this when they say, "I'm too tired to exercise after a long day at work!") While this sounds logical, biologically it doesn't hold up. Let's explore why by going back to our car analogy. What happens when you don't drive your car for months on end? It probably won't start.

I know this because I learned the same thing happens with motorcycles. One fall, I forgot to remove the battery from my motorcycle before cold weather set in. I didn't consider the effect the Boston winter would have on the battery while my motorcycle sat motionless from October to April. I shouldn't have been surprised to find a completely dead battery when I tried to ride the bike on the first gorgeous spring day. Running the motor recharges the battery, which keeps it ready to fire the motor into action.

Our bodies are similar. When we are physically active, we do expend energy but the exercise also "recharges" our batteries by strengthening and activating our muscles, joints, and organs.

When you're almost anxious, exercise brings many other positive effects. In one study, for example, thirty sedentary women who had generalized anxiety participated in a program that involved lifting weights or cycling twice a week. At the end of the six-week program, 60 percent of the women in the weight-lifting group and 40 percent of the women in the cycling group had remission of their anxiety symptoms. They also had significant reductions in worry symptoms compared with women in the control group, who didn't exercise.[14]

One of the most impressive conclusions from this study is that exercise is helpful even at not-so-vigorous intensities. Simply moving at a moderate pace significantly reduces anxiety. Furthermore, researchers have found that people can benefit from even a relatively brief exercise program. In one review of earlier studies, researchers determined that exercise programs lasting no longer than twelve weeks were effective at reducing anxiety symptoms.[15] You don't have to be cycling 100 miles a week or bench-pressing your weight to see improvements in your almost anxiety.

For most of my patients, one of the major roadblocks to

starting an exercise routine is their overestimation of just how much activity they need to do. Jenny, for example, would say things like this:

- "I don't have enough time to exercise."
- "I have to work out too long in order for it to count."

All of these beliefs got Jenny stuck even more deeply in her almost anxiety. They also increased her troubled eating patterns, since she would start to get anxious about her lack of exercise, which actually made her eat more.

The truth is, people will *always* face challenges when trying to add new commitments to their already busy lives, especially an activity that can trigger negative thoughts (such as "I'm already tired—why wear myself down into sweaty exhaustion?"). But if you don't incorporate exercise into your life, your almost anxiety is likely to continue.

Here's how to make room in your life for more activity:

- **Remember that you don't have to go overboard!** How much exercise do you need? Although experts have weighed in with very different recommendations, I hold with the U.S. Surgeon General's suggestion of at least 150 minutes of moderate-intensity physical activity per week for adults; this means as little as 30 minutes a day, five days a week.[16] *Moderate* intensity means a level that would allow you to carry on a conversation while you're exercising without gasping for breath.

- **Start with activities you like.** Exercise can be challenging enough without diving into an activity you don't even enjoy. So before becoming more active (which is the term

I prefer to use when discussing exercise), make a list of activities that you already know you like. Jenny enjoyed tai chi, which is where she started when she got back into physical activity. Make your list as realistic and pleasurable as possible. Also, try to come up with diverse activities that meet different needs, such as walking around a mall (when the weather is bad), joining an exercise group at work (for socializing), checking out workout DVDs from the library (for a free form of exercise), and joining a gym with early and late hours (to accommodate your busy schedule). But keep in mind that for some people, exercising late at night can interfere with sleep. So try out different times and track them to ensure that your exercise routine does not come at the cost of your sleep.

- **Start small.** It's nearly impossible to change your habits overnight. As I was writing this book, I wanted to make sure that I stayed active, but at first I kept bumping up against the time constraints of adding this project to my full-time job. One of the strategies that helped me get unstuck was to break up my activity routine into smaller, less time-consuming goals that I could still meet despite the time crunch. For example, I kept my yoga mat out in my apartment, so if I couldn't make it to class, I would still do a few yoga poses at night to unwind. Also, when I was tired, instead of going for a five-mile jog, I would make a deal with myself to just go for twenty minutes while listening to some of my favorite music. By decreasing the time commitment, I was able to stay engaged in physical activity even though my schedule was tight.

- **Set goals.** Most people get their work done, do their grocery shopping, and throw their laundry into the washer and dryer every week, but many have a much harder time staying active. If this sounds like you, a great way to get started is to set measureable goals. For example, in addition to doing tai chi twice a week, Jenny committed to taking the stairs up to her sixth-floor office every day. Even a *little* more physical activity is better than none when it comes to reducing your almost anxiety.

- **Monitor your progress.** Recording your activity helps reinforce your behavior and increases your motivation to stick with it. Although you can get fancy with your tracking system, simply putting a note on your calendar every time you exercise will do. I would also suggest that you track your anxiety level pre- and post-activity. I personally started to exercise more once I noticed that my general anxiety levels were much lower after a jog around the block, even when I started out tired.

- **Bring a friend.** James Fowler, PhD, co-author of the book *Connected*, asked a TED conference audience this question: "Are your friends making you fat?" Based on his and others' research, he concluded that if you're more active, you're more likely to hang out with friends who are also active, which propels you to exercise more. However, the opposite is also true: the more sedentary you are, the more likely you are to have friends who are couch potatoes. After reading his work, I enlisted one of my close friends to be my exercise buddy. She and I agree that Dr. Fowler's research is consistent with our own experience: by having each other to run with, we were able to start a jogging routine that ultimately led us to run a 10K race (which wasn't even our original goal). So to help you get your batteries recharged, look for a reliable support person who also wants to get moving.

Jenny's Outcome

As I do with most of my patients, I encouraged Jenny to make one change at a time. Since her first challenge was to get a handle on her eating, for the first few weeks we worked together to help her find healthier foods and to eat smaller meals more frequently.

At first, Jenny resisted eating breakfast, saying that she was never hungry in the morning. Yet, when she tracked her eating, she found that skipping breakfast led her to stuff herself with bigger meals later in the day. So we started small. Jenny eventually agreed to have a piece of fruit as soon as she woke up. By tracking her anxiety levels before and after meals, Jenny discovered that her body seemed to "run smoother" when she ate breakfast. She was also surprised to find that she was less hungry at lunchtime, enabling her to make healthier choices about midday portion sizes.

In terms of exercising, Jenny liked the idea of leading a more active life rather than exercising with the goal of losing weight. We brainstormed ways to increase her general activity level, starting with tai chi and trips up the stairs at work. After six weeks, Jenny joined a gym with a swimming pool, which she associated with fun childhood memories instead of hard work. Her goal was to swim just once a week at first, usually on Sunday morning. Slowly, Jenny integrated more physical activities into her daily schedule. And because the changes were small, she was able to stick with them.

Jenny's final challenge was to improve her sleep. Her worries had been keeping her awake, but she didn't like the idea of practicing my sleep hygiene suggestions, as she found them too intrusive on her routine. Yet, Jenny knew that without more restful sleep, she would have trouble maintaining her new eating and exercise habits, given that she ate more and exercised less when she was tired.

Jenny slowly developed more regular sleep patterns. The main challenge for her was to find ways to arrange her life around her natural sleep cycle. To that end, she was fortunate to be able to negotiate more flexible work hours so she could come in to the office later in the morning (and stay later at work) to accommodate her natural tendency to stay up late at night.

While Jenny was working with me, she also noticed that she had become isolated and enjoyed fewer friendships than when she was in college. So we also addressed the power of strong social networks for relieving almost anxiety. I'll discuss this issue in the next chapter.

❖

8

Tapping Into the Power of Your Social Network

The winter morning was crisp yet filled with enthusiasm, joy, and love as my neighbors Aimee and Eric, my boyfriend David, and I hopped into my car to drive to New York City.

We were visiting my close friend Lara for a holiday brunch. Lara had been diagnosed with breast cancer earlier in the year and had just finished all of her treatments. Finally, she was deemed "cancer free." She had requested the presence of her close network of friends to help her celebrate the milestone.

Like a lot of people in large metro areas, Lara had recently moved to the city. She had barely settled into her new life and job when she was diagnosed. But she used social networking tools to keep her old friends involved in her life. Immediately after the diagnosis, her girlfriends created a Facebook group, called "The Journey," so that those close to Lara could follow her progress. On any given day, either Lara was posting how the latest surgery or treatment was affecting her or one of us was updating the anxious support network.

During her first surgery, Lara was surrounded not only by family, including her mother and father, but also her close friends, all of whom stepped into the rotating vigil at times of need. Lara found a way to have a friend with her at most, if not at all, of her chemotherapy treatments.

I appreciated one of Lara's natural strengths: her ability to tap into the power of her social networks. And now here we were during the holiday season celebrating her survival.

Nearly twenty people filled her cozy one-bedroom apartment for the Sunday brunch. Tears flowed while we spoke about Lara's strength during the storm of her cancer, the value of what each of us had learned in supporting her, and how another chapter in her life was about to begin. In that apartment, it dawned on me that I was witnessing in real time the many benefits that research on social support shows.

The experience left me wondering how some people, like Lara, can tap so powerfully into their social support while others, like many of my patients with almost anxiety, fall into isolation and end up missing out on the exact "medicine" that could help cure what ails them.

In sharp contrast to Lara's experience stands Nafisseh's struggle with isolation, avoidance, and finding social support.

Nafisseh's Story

Nafisseh, a quiet woman, became my patient in her mid-twenties. Her family immigrated to the United States from Iran when she was young, landing in the suburbs of Los Angeles.

Her transition to America took place during her teenage

years, which were already a challenging time in her development. Overnight, she was transported from a society where women were often oppressed to the halls of an American high school, where young women took pride in expressing themselves in every possible way. Nafisseh wasn't used to their clothes, cosmetics, cars, and customs. As an only child, she had no siblings to help her process this experience.

She tried to fit in for two years but ended up feeling more and more isolated, which led her to drop out of school and take a job at the local library.

Working at the library suited Nafisseh well. She spent as much time filing books as possible, which allowed her to stay away from patrons and gave her more time to read. Nafisseh's parents weren't concerned about her isolation, merely thinking she was "shy." After a few years, her life consisted of work at the library, time with her mother, and weekends reading alone. Nafisseh knew a few women who also worked at the library, but she only considered them acquaintances at best, and she would politely refuse their friendly invitations to social events.

One day, as we were discussing why she avoided people, Nafisseh recalled an event from years before: while talking to a male history teacher in high school, she had a panic attack. She wasn't sure what started it, but she vividly remembered the classroom spinning, followed by feelings of dizziness, shortness of breath, and nausea. The teacher walked her to the nurse's office, who kept an eye on her until her mother came to pick her up. The nurse told Nafisseh's mom that perhaps she'd had a panic attack, but that did not register with her mother's own cultural beliefs. Instead, Nafisseh's mom suspected she had a cold or a stomach virus and kept her at home for the rest of the week.

Nafisseh recalled the great sense of relief she felt while she was at home that week, where she didn't have to face the "different American kids." But she also remembered her anxiety, and even feelings of terror, over having to go back to school the next Monday.

Nafisseh was feeling *anticipatory anxiety*. As you may recall, anticipatory anxiety makes it harder to face your fears. She recalled crying when she had to return to school, afraid that she would have the same sensations again when she saw the history teacher. To avoid those feelings, she convinced her mother to ask the school to take her out of the history course and put her in another class. Although this might seem like a reasonable approach to reduce her anxiety, it only further cemented Nafisseh's belief that she wouldn't be able to tolerate panic-like sensations if they occurred again.

Eventually Nafisseh's life became so secluded that she started to feel sad. She wouldn't call it *depression*, since she didn't feel like she had the right to be depressed, given how lucky she "should" feel about living in the United States versus Iran.

Feeling sad likely further contributed to Nafisseh's social isolation. Yet, when I asked her how she managed to survive without any friends, she looked surprised. "But I do have friends— they are all in Iran." She indeed had stayed in touch with her friends back home. She felt a strong sense of connection with them and explained that they understood her in a way that her American peers never would. But maintaining close ties with these friends on the other side of the world kept her cut off from her current life.

I first met Nafisseh after she moved from Los Angeles to Boston to live with an aunt, who had been concerned over the years about the young woman's isolation. The aunt, Nadia, had also immigrated to the United States from Iran, taking a job as a bank teller, marrying a local man, and having two daughters.

Nadia was well connected with the Iranian community in Boston and had built a close-knit social support network. Her daughters, who were younger than Nafisseh, also had a great group of friends.

Nadia's strong social connection stood in sharp contrast to Nafisseh's isolation. Nadia sought me out and asked if I would meet with Nafisseh to help her "get integrated" into American life.

When I first assessed Nafisseh, her clinical presentation and symptoms didn't meet the criteria for a diagnosis of any anxiety disorders. She held a job, didn't completely avoid people in social situations, and had met one person she liked in Boston through her aunt. Although she was still slightly anxious in social situations, she wanted more friends but felt like she had never learned how to make them. Given this picture, I thought she had the almost anxious social type. She was bordering on a diagnosis of social anxiety disorder, but not yet there.

I also assessed Nafisseh for panic disorder, given her notable panic attack in high school. Right after the attack, she reported feeling fearful about having another one, but that had subsided over the years. She hadn't felt this fear in quite some time. If I had seen Nafisseh closer to the incident, her panic symptoms might have been severe enough to warrant a diagnosis of panic disorder. But currently, that wasn't the case.

This is an important caveat: although you might have an *almost* level of symptoms right now, at some point your symptoms could become severe enough to meet a diagnosis for a clinical disorder. On the other hand, anxiety disorders can have a natural remission, so if you've had a diagnosis of panic disorder in your life, you might not currently meet the clinical diagnosis for it.

Despite dropping out of high school, Nafisseh was an intelligent, astute young woman. The sharp contrast she saw between her teen years and her cousins' lives helped her realize that if she could find a way to create a social network while also facing some of her fears, she might feel more involved in the world around her.

Nafisseh had recently started to dream of getting her GED and perhaps attending college. She also wanted to think about dating so she could one day have a family of her own. To meet these goals, Nafisseh knew she would have to change the way she was approaching her life.

Social Support: A Natural Motivator

Lara and Nafisseh seem to fall at the opposite ends of the social-connectedness spectrum. Lara built and nurtured a strong social network in her day-to-day life, and she was able to tap into its power in her time of need. Nafisseh, however, not only lacked such a network; she wasn't able to make friends, either in high school or with library co-workers.

Research points to the benefits of Lara's type of network and the harms of Nafisseh's type of isolation. Researchers who study the positive impact of social support on mental health have two hypotheses for why this association exists. Some think that social support exerts a direct effect on individuals' over-all sense of well-being (main effect), while other researchers believe that social support exerts an indirect effect by helping people cope with stressful life events (called stress-buffering effect).[1] Lara's story is a great example of the stress-buffering hypothesis. When she was diagnosed with cancer, it's likely that her initial concerns about how she'd get through the cancer treatments were relieved by her knowledge that she'd have plenty of friends and family to encourage her during the difficult times. These social contacts also provided help by taking her to doctor appointments and bringing food to her apartment when she felt too weak to accomplish these tasks on her own.

Nafisseh, on the other hand, didn't get the sense that she belonged with the people around her. As such, she didn't have a network to tap into during her stressful teen years (except for the friends who were far away and her parents, who didn't see her isolation as a problem). Dealing with her anxiety on her own, she resorted to avoidance to try to manage it. Avoidance, as you've learned, will only get you stuck further in your anxiety.

Avoidance also often leads to *more* social isolation, either real or perceived. Perceived social isolation, or loneliness, is a strong predictor of a wide range of negative psychological and medical outcomes. For example, feeling lonely has been related to these issues:[2]

- depressive symptoms
- drug use
- obesity
- elevated blood pressure

Additionally, a 2010 study found that after stressful life events (such as the death of a loved one, divorce, or job loss), people who had higher-than-average social support from a friend were 30 percent less likely to experience psychological distress.[3]

More specific to our subject here, the same study found that people who had a high level of social support from a relative were 80 percent less likely to develop panic disorder in the aftermath of a stressful life event. On the other hand, conflict in close relationships, such as with your spouse, is associated with an increased risk for a clinical diagnosis of many disorders, including generalized anxiety disorder, panic disorder, major depressive disorder, and alcohol problems.[4]

Social support is also important during happy times in our lives. Sharing a happy event with a close other is called "capitalizing," and it has been linked to an increase in positive emotions above and beyond those generated by the event itself.[5] Furthermore, research suggests that the degree of support from a romantic partner following a positive event is more predictive of long-term relationship satisfaction than degree of support following a negative event.[6] Thus, it is important to nurture your social support network in both good times and bad.

No matter how the light of social support strikes the multifaceted diamond of mental health, you will find a strong association. In short, *having more perceived social support is almost always a buffer against mental health problems. A lack of social support (real or perceived) is associated with worse mental and physical health.* Isolation and loneliness not only hurt you; they can also have a spillover effect on those around you.

Emotions Spread through Social Supports

Encouragement can spread through a social network—but so can loneliness. In a recent study, John Cacioppo and colleagues looked at data from the Framingham Heart Study to see how lonely people could affect those in their social network.[7] The question was, to use our current example: If Nafisseh felt lonely, would she be more likely to attract friends who were also lonely? They called this the *"homophily"* hypothesis (think of the phrase "birds of a feather flock together"). Or would she cause others in her social network to feel lonely? They called this the *induction* hypothesis. They also tested the *shared environment* hypothesis, which would suggest that the environmental experience shared by individuals contributes to their feelings of loneliness.

Results from this study were consistent with the induction hypothesis, suggesting that loneliness spreads from person to person within a social network, like a contagious cold. Furthermore, the researchers found that this association was stronger for friends who lived close together, specifically within a mile of each other, and that it was true for up to three levels of association. This means that if Lara, my friend who survived breast cancer, were to feel lonely for an extended period of time, it would increase not only the chance that I would feel lonely but that one of my other friends might also feel lonely.

Similar studies have shown that happiness, smoking, and obesity also spread through social networks.[8]

All of these studies suggest that those around us have a strong impact on our physical and emotional health. This impact is not limited to those close to you, like your family; your friends can also significantly alter the course of your life.

So, although your social network is powerful in getting you unstuck while you are almost anxious, it can also cause negative feelings such as loneliness to spread. While you're thinking about improving your social network, then, it makes sense to give some thought to *who* is in it!

. . .

In summary, to tame your anxiety and make it work for you, it is paramount that you learn to find help within your social support network. In addition, most people can benefit from increasing the breadth and depth of their network.

Social support usually becomes even more important while you're doing the work described in upcoming chapters on developing new skills, such as facing your fears. For many of the people I see who are almost anxious, the idea of doing the exact thing they've been avoiding is scary. You likely will need to call on your friends and loved ones when you approach your fears, which is a crucial part of addressing almost anxiety.

Now is a good time for you to take a closer look at your social network to assess how strong and beneficial it is to your well-being.

The MSPSS: A Measure for Checking Your Support Network

As you consider your social network and gauge how helpful it will be for reducing your almost anxiety, please answer the questions on the Multidimensional Scale of Perceived Social Support (MSPSS) in exercise 16.[9] You can also download this exercise at www.AlmostAnxious.com. This tool is widely used in the mental health field to measure support from your significant others, family, and friends.

Your scores are interpreted as averages. Higher values mean you have more support in that area.

Exercise 16.

The Multidimensional Scale of Perceived Social Support

Read each statement carefully; then indicate how you feel about each statement, with scores ranging from 1 ("very strongly disagree") to 7 ("very strongly agree").

	Very Strongly Disagree	Strongly Disagree	Mildly Disagree	Neutral	Mildly Agree	Strongly Agree	Very Strongly Agree	My Score
	1	2	3	4	5	6	7	
1.	There is a special person who is around when I am in need.							
2.	There is a special person with whom I can share my joys and sorrows.							
3.	My family really tries to help me.							
4.	I get the emotional help and support I need from my family.							
5.	I have a special person who is a real source of comfort to me.							
6.	My friends really try to help me.							
7.	I can count on my friends when things go wrong.							
8.	I can talk about my problems with my family.							
9.	I have friends with whom I can share my joys and sorrows.							
10.	There is a special person in my life who cares about my feelings.							
11.	My family is willing to help me make decisions.							
12.	I can talk about my problems with my friends.							

To calculate your scores on each of the subscales, add the scores from the following questions and then divide by four.

- **Family subscale:**
  Add the results from questions
  3, 4, 8, and 11; then divide by 4 = _____

- **Friends subscale:**
  Add the results from questions
  6, 7, 9, and 12; then divide by 4 = _____

- **Significant other subscale:**
  Add the results from questions
  1, 2, 5, and 10; then divide by 4 = _____

- **Total scale:**
  Add the results of all questions;
  then divide by 12 = _____

What do your MSPSS scores mean? Research on the MSPSS, which has been studied across disorders, generally supports a negative relationship between social support and mental health problems, with lower perceived social support related to higher levels of anxiety and depression. The table in figure 15 shows MSPSS scores for four groups of people: students and people who have depression, cancer, and social anxiety disorder (SAD).[10] Although there are no ideal scores, you can compare your scores with the student sample, which on average is considered healthy, versus those who are depressed and might be struggling with their support network or lack thereof. Pay particular attention to your lowest score, as this may be an area where you need to focus the most attention.

Figure 15.
MSPSS Study Comparison Scores

MSPSS Subscale	Student Sample[11]	Depression[12]	Cancer[13]	SAD[14]
Family	5.54	4.05	6.27	3.94
Friends	5.17	4.20	2.58	3.75
Significant Others	5.56	4.69	6.44	4.34

Nafisseh received the following scores on the MSPSS:

- Family = 4.9
- Friends = 3.7
- Significant other = 2.8

Since all of her scores were on the low end of the spectrum, I think Nafisseh made the right decision in seeking outside help to learn how to create, and then capitalize on, a support network. As you might have predicted, her score was the highest on the family subscale, since that was her primary source of support, but *very* low on the friends and significant others subscales.

When Nafisseh had this baseline data in hand, we set to work on building and tapping into a social support system. Here are some tips on how you can do the same.

Map Your Network with a Social Support Matrix

Now that you know the overall strength of your social support network, the next step is to better understand it by making a map of it.

Although Nafisseh had 300 Facebook friends, she did not

have many people she would consider *close* friends. However, she could name many acquaintances whom she would not necessarily rely on for support but whom she liked. What's more, she felt that if she wanted to get closer to them, they would welcome it.

I asked Nafisseh to take a look at the graph in figure 16. This graphic contains concentric circles, each representing levels of relationship. The inner circles contain your closest friends and family, while the outer edges hold the names of those you might consider acquaintances. In the family section of Nafisseh's social matrix, she was able to name three people: her mom, her aunt Nadia, and a cousin.

As we broadened her perspective, Nafisseh realized she would be able to rely on a few other family members, so she added them. In contrast, when I asked her to name people whom she could rely on in the friend slice of her matrix, she listed only one close friend in her inner network, and the rest were acquaintances who went further toward the edge of the matrix.

As Nafisseh put names into her social matrix, we were able to visually identify areas where she needed to invest energy toward building her network and areas where she had support but did not capitalize on it.

As you picture the people around you sorted into groups, what does your social network matrix look like? Who is your closest support and who is in the acquaintance groups?

My Social Support Network

Take a few moments to write down the names of the people whom you draw your social support from in each of the categories. Move from close, intimate relationships in the center to people you are friendly with and acquaintances in the outer rings of the circle. In each category, try to come up with as many names as possible. Even if you haven't relied on particular people recently, but you know that they would be there for you, write their names down.

Figure 16.
Nafisseh's Social Network

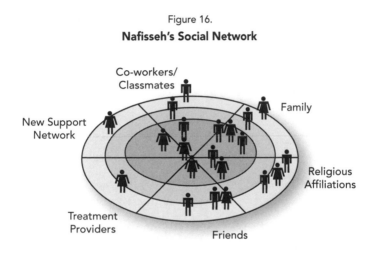

Social Support Networks Can Change

When Lara was first diagnosed with cancer, she had a large network of family, friends, and co-workers (so many that she may have had trouble staying connected to some of them). As she progressed through her cancer treatment, she noticed a dramatic change in the number of people around her: the *quantity* of friends seemed to decrease, but the strength of the friendships that remained was more powerful. At this time in her life, Lara focused more on the inner circles of her social support network, since her energy was limited.

The research seems to agree with our intuitive sense that

the quality, not the quantity, of social relationships is most important for our well-being. For example, one study of college students demonstrated that participants' *satisfaction* with their social support system, but not the *size* of their social support system, was predictive of both improved physical and mental health.[15]

Using the Power of Your Social Support Network

The people around you are going to be pivotal in helping you overcome your almost anxiety for many reasons. First, it is likely that your loved ones are in the best position to help you identify when your almost anxiety is becoming a problem, given that they are with you most often and likely knew you before your anxiety reached the "almost" level. Second, your loved ones probably want to help you.

But odds are also good that they don't know exactly how to help you. Often, I see loved ones who dismiss the concern (like Nafisseh's parents did), not because they don't care, but because they don't think it's a serious problem or because there's a stigma associated with it.

Alternatively, I encounter loved ones who are very involved in my patients' lives, doing whatever they possibly can to help the person get better. Unfortunately, there is a fine line between being *helpful* and *enabling*—the kind of "support" that actually leads to more anxiety. When loved ones do something to help people who are almost anxious, such as taking their kids to school because they're scared of driving, they may actually be enabling the avoidance and thus fostering even more anxiety.

Still, it's understandable why a loved one would want to do anything to get you to feel better. After all, none of us enjoys seeing the people we love in distress. So what is your loved one to do? Below is a list of dos and don'ts for family members and other loved ones who want to partner up with you to tackle your almost anxiety.

Dos and Don'ts for Loved Ones Who Want to Help with Your Almost Anxiety

Dos

- Learn: The more you know about your loved one's almost anxiety, the better a helper you will become.

- Motivate: Cheerlead! Your loved one will need your help to fight the avoidance.

- Challenge: Create a contract with your loved one asking for ways that you can challenge him or her in recovering from almost anxiety. Much as a good personal trainer helps you keep going in the gym when you are tired, you can help your loved one keep approaching—not avoiding— feared situations.

- Support: Provide emotional and tangible support, but make sure to ask what is most helpful. One way to be helpful is to read this book and assist your loved one through the journey of overcoming avoidance.

Don'ts

- Enable: This is actually a form of avoidance. It may temporarily ease your loved one's anxiety, but over the long term, it just prolongs the problem.

- Provide reassurance: Reassurance is yet another form of avoidance. Much like enabling, it will only brew more anxiety.

- Criticize: Sometimes it can be challenging to understand the magnitude of almost anxiety and the difficulty your loved one has in facing his or her fears, which in turn might lead you to criticize. This will only hinder your relationship and get your loved one further stuck.

When Nafisseh first moved to Boston, her aunt often reassured her that she shouldn't worry about her lack of social interactions and that there was nothing awkward about her. Unfortunately, the reassurance was only momentarily helpful, and after a while Nafisseh started to worry again. As a result, *that* type of support wasn't helpful.

As we worked together, Nafisseh learned how this reassurance felt good for a brief time but ultimately kept her stuck. So Nafisseh asked her aunt to help her *approach* fearful things instead of merely reassuring her that all was okay.

You might ask close family members and friends to read this book so they can better understand how almost anxiety works and the kind of support you need from them.

Boosting Your Social Support When It's Scarce

Nafisseh was stuck: she'd just moved to a new city where she didn't know many people, after already being lonely for years in familiar surroundings. Her almost anxiety fell within the panic and social types, both of which can be associated with social isolation. Thus, Nafisseh was fighting multiple fronts at once. To help her get unstuck, we followed several of the same steps that I recommend for you below:

- **Create a social support matrix:** If you haven't done this yet, take some time and write down the names of people who will be your support system as you learn to tame your almost anxiety.

- **Engage and capitalize on existing supports:** Approach the people from the different areas of your matrix, share your almost anxiety story, and ask if they are willing to help you in your journey to overcome avoidance.

- **Be specific about the types of help you need:** For example, Nafisseh asked to join her aunt's book club. Her aunt also agreed to host a holiday party and invite her broader social network to help Nafisseh meet new people. In Lara's case, she created a Facebook calendar where we could sign up to accompany her to chemotherapy appointments. What do you think your friends could do that would help you reduce your almost anxiety? (Remember, they shouldn't be enabling your avoidance!)

- **Create new support systems:** With many of my patients who are almost anxious, our work is focused on creating a social support network from scratch, rather than leveraging an existing one. Here are some ideas that they have found helpful:

  - *Activities you enjoy:* One way to make new friends is to participate in activities you enjoy that are social. *Talk* to people at these gatherings. (This may seem obvious, but it's a step that many of my patients haven't already done.) Nafisseh loved cooking, so she signed up for a cooking class that allowed her to meet others with a similar passion. One way to do this is to look at adult continuing education programs at local colleges, libraries, and community organizations such as the YMCA.

Often such programs offer a wide range of activities that they list online.

- *Activities you have always wanted to try:* Getting out of your own comfort zone is important if you are to over-come avoidance and isolation. Nafisseh enjoyed taking pictures but had never devoted time to getting better at it. She learned about Meetup, which is a website that many of my patients and friends use to try new activi-ties. The site lists groups in cities and towns that are devoted to particular activities. Nafisseh signed up for a "photography tour" of Boston. This group encour-aged strangers to come together to discuss the process of taking pictures. Then as a group, they wandered through the city photographing monuments and his-toric sites.

- *Being patient:* Regardless of how you choose to widen your social support system, remember that just as it took time to become socially isolated, it will take time to build new relationships. Stick with it. Only by put-ting yourself out in the world and opening yourself up to other people, over and over, can you deepen your relationships with others.

Nafisseh's Outcome

After exploring many activities, Nafisseh settled into two dif-ferent social circles with people whose company she enjoyed: a book club and a photography group. Once she became com-fortable interacting with all these individuals, she started think-ing about dating. Eventually she created an online profile on a dating web site. All of these experiences were difficult at first;

she often wanted to give up when she felt like she was doing something "wrong" in social situations, or she worried that people thought she was weird. Nafisseh even had a panic attack during one of her first dating attempts.

But she stuck with it. She had mapped out whom she could turn to for help, then relied on her family and friends to encourage her to keep approaching her fears instead of avoiding them. She and I also kept working in our sessions to change her behaviors and ways of thinking related to her almost anxiety. Nafisseh's social support network kept her anchored while she learned the skills that I'll discuss in the next chapter.

❖

9

Challenge Your Anxiety-Fueled Way of Thinking

When we begin to establish patterns of anxiety avoidance, our thinking can become distorted and make changing these avoidance behaviors more difficult, as Eduardo's story demonstrates.

Eduardo's Story

Eduardo was having a good time at a work-related party when a panic attack struck. He was sixty years old when it happened, and only now at sixty-five did he come to discuss it with me.

Eduardo had always been gregarious, and he'd built a large network of friends, colleagues, and acquaintances. He was married with two adult children and worked as a manager at a local restaurant, where he had first started as a waiter twenty years ago. Eduardo thrived in the social scene of the restaurant, telling me, "Working at the restaurant is like being home in Puerto Rico. People are always socializing. We are all *familia*." He knew the restaurant's regulars by name, always going the extra mile to make them feel like they were part of his extended family.

Given how outgoing Eduardo had always been and how much he enjoyed his job, it was completely surreal to him that he had a panic attack in the very place where he'd always felt at home. He was talking to the restaurant owner when it started. The first thing Eduardo noticed was his heart beating faster. He immediately thought, "That's strange; am I having a heart attack?" As the conversation continued, Eduardo began feeling panic-like symptoms: dizziness, numbness and tingling in his hands and legs, and finally a sense that he was leaving his own body. "You okay, *hermano*? You look white as a ghost," the owner said. In response, Eduardo excused himself to go to the restroom.

"That is when things got even worse. As I went into the restroom, the room began to spin, and I felt really dizzy and nauseated. I called my wife, who is a psychiatric nurse, to see if I was having a heart attack," he explained. By listening carefully to his symptoms, his wife, Maria, realized that Eduardo was probably having a panic attack.

Instead of feeling relieved, Eduardo got mad at his wife, accusing her of dismissing his symptoms. As he put it, "I thought only crazy people had anxiety attacks." Eduardo eventually rejoined the party for a few moments before excusing himself and taking a cab home; he refused to drive in case he was indeed having a heart attack.

The first thing he did the next day was to schedule a check-up with his primary care doctor. Maria was frustrated, since she was almost positive that Eduardo had had a panic attack, but she went along with his plan. After a battery of tests and a consultation with a cardiologist, Eduardo's doctors assured him that he did not have a heart condition and that his wife was likely correct with her suspicion of a panic attack. Eduardo felt relief over the test results for a few weeks, but his heart-related fears kept plaguing him.

At my first meeting with Eduardo and Maria, he told me that his life had never been the same since the panic attack. Although Eduardo did not avoid the restaurant or stop working, he felt as if he was always worried about the possibility of having another panic attack or, even worse, an actual heart attack. At work, Eduardo would notice that he was often more distracted by thoughts like "What if I lose control? . . . What if I go crazy? . . . What if I get sick and cannot get help?" These "what if" thoughts plagued Eduardo and robbed him of the joy he used to experience at the restaurant. The thoughts also got him stuck on his own almost anxious hamster wheel.

Eduardo also avoided some situations in response to the panic attack. He noticed that he would remember the attack when he was at parties. At first, he was reluctant to go to gatherings at all, but Maria insisted they continue their social life. So he would try to make an appearance, then leave. While he was there, he'd avoid alcohol, because he was afraid of the "out-of-control" feeling it gave him.

It was at Maria's request that Eduardo ended up in my office. He'd regularly ask her to check his heart rate and to agree that he was "not crazy." Eduardo told me that in his mind only the "crazy people my wife works with" had anxiety attacks. He was ashamed and embarrassed by this thought. At first, Maria was happy to be supportive and reassure her husband that he was okay, but after a while, she grew frustrated. Five years later, she was fed up and told Eduardo to seek professional help, as her reassurance was not helping him.

Eduardo's symptoms were at the edge of a clinical diagnosis of panic disorder, but he was still within the almost anxious realm, given that he continued to enjoy most of his life and did not restrict many of his activities. However, I was sure that if Maria had not been strongly encouraging him to face his fears, Eduardo would have developed full-blown panic disorder.

The "what if" thoughts that Eduardo experienced are not limited to people with panic-like sensations. Most people, at some point in their lives, are bothered by catastrophic, distorted thoughts that cause them to momentarily lose focus on reality.

Errors in Thinking Can Fuel Anxiety

As you have learned, avoidance maintains your anxiety and makes it more difficult to face anxiety-provoking situations.

By avoiding, you start to see danger in situations that shouldn't be worrisome, such as a trip to the grocery store, simply because the last time you went to the store, you felt anxiety. As such, you pair grocery shopping with anxious feelings, and as a result you stop going to the store. By avoiding the supermarket, you start to believe that the store is indeed dangerous, which then leads to more distorted thinking and more avoidance. Eventually, you stop challenging the anxious thought of "Grocery shopping causes me to feel anxious," and you start to believe this thought as reality. This is the point—when you accept that anxious thoughts are reality, you get stuck.

In many ways, almost anxiety is like wearing prescription

glasses that are either too strong or too weak. Your thoughts are filtered through these lenses, making your surroundings seem distorted and blurry. I am not saying you need to replace anxious thoughts with happy thoughts, as though you were wearing rose-colored glasses. But it is crucial to examine your thoughts, with the ultimate goal of finding a more balanced way of thinking that is not guided primarily by your almost anxiety.

In chapter 5 you learned how to separate your thoughts from your feelings. The exercises you completed in that chapter will be useful now. The main goal in this chapter will be to learn how to examine your anxious thoughts, with two main questions in mind:

- Are these thoughts valid?
- Are these thoughts helpful in coping with the situation I'm facing?

Such questions are at the core of cognitive-behavioral therapy, which has been shown to be helpful in the treatment of anxiety disorders.

Identify and Challenge Your Distorted Thoughts

All of us are thinking all the time. In fact, a chain of thoughts is always going through the average human's mind, often in a nonlinear fashion: "What do I have to do next? What will I do this weekend? How will I finish my work-related tasks by the deadline? Will I have enough time to cook dinner tonight? How will I find my perfect mate? Will I ever have kids? Will I be able to pay my bills this month?"

Thoughts are so free-flowing and continuous that most people don't really pay close attention to them, except when the thoughts start to interfere with their lives, either by creating negative feelings (anxiety, sadness, and so on) or by distorting their reality. We all, at one time or another, assume that a *thought* is the same thing as a *fact*.

For example, many people may say something like, "I feel anxious because I am sure my boss is not satisfied with my work." This sentence has two parts: feelings (I'm anxious) and a thought (my boss is dissatisfied with my work). But is that thought irrational or unreasonable? Is it distorted? How do you identify whether your thoughts are actually the root cause for your almost anxiety?

First, you'll need to broaden your reality by challenging your specific patterns of thinking. Here are four steps to identifying distorted thinking.

Step 1: Notice Your Mood and Physical Sensations
The first step in identifying a distorted, unbalanced thought is to examine how you are feeling (including mood and physical sensations). Often, it is much easier to assess your mood than your exact thoughts. Individuals who are more panic-sensitive might first notice a sudden change in their bodily sensations before they recognize a change in their thoughts.

For example, Eduardo often noticed his heart pounding a little faster, which would immediately trigger a feeling of anxiety or danger. (If you are still struggling with differentiating between your thoughts and feelings, you may want to review chapter 5.) As soon as you notice a change in either your mood or your bodily sensations, move on to step 2.

Step 2: Write Down Your Thoughts Related to the Anxiety
Identifying your thoughts that are related to a mood change is

a skill that takes practice to develop. As soon as Eduardo's heart skipped a beat, he would think, "What if I am having a heart attack?" On my Yosemite hike, I thought, "What if I plunge to my death?"

At this stage, I encourage you to write down the most simple, naked version of your thought. Often, when I ask patients what they were thinking, they tend to give me a paragraph full of thoughts and feelings, which is helpful but will not aid in challenging a specific thought. Identifying the basic thought is particularly tricky since we don't generally have one single thought that exists on its own.

So when you notice anxious feelings, you might have a sequence of many thoughts: "What if I have a heart attack? What is wrong with me? Why am I so anxious when my boss looks at me? If I die now, what would happen to my family?" Write all of these thoughts down, but as you move to step 3, be prepared to work with one thought at a time.

When most of my patients begin observing and writing down their thoughts, they notice that a handful of thoughts show up again and again. Much like Eduardo, many of my patients who are almost anxious have numerous "what if" thoughts.

Step 3: Label the Distortions in Your Thoughts

When you have identified a few distorted thoughts, label them by the specific way that they're distorted. Psychologists have created a list of "cognitive distortions" that apply to most unbalanced thoughts that someone with almost anxiety might experience. Labeling your thoughts as a distortion will help you challenge them. It also provides further evidence that these thoughts might be at the root of your almost anxiety.

The following is a list of the classic types of distortions common among people with all forms of almost anxiety. Keep in mind that even though I am separating them by almost subtypes, you will likely have thoughts that fall within each of the categories. Some especially tricky thoughts might even fall into more than one category, and that's okay. The key here is to identify any aspect of your thoughts that might be distorted.

COMMON DISTORTIONS ACROSS ALL
ALMOST ANXIETY TYPES

Emotional reasoning: Often, when you engage in emotional reasoning, you are using your emotions to interpret reality. Remember the blurry prescription glasses? These are usually the culprit when it comes to emotional reasoning. For example, you might say, "I feel anxious; therefore this situation is dangerous." But when you say, "I feel anxious," you are identifying an emotion (anxiety), not describing a thought. If your sentence starts with "I feel . . . ," it is likely emotional reasoning. Similar emotional reasoning thoughts might be "I am anxious; therefore I will mess up this talk, or everyone will think I am a horrible speaker, or I am a terrible parent." All of these thoughts have a common denominator: they use your anxiety to interpret a situation as problematic.

Personalizing: In this type of distortion, you take anything someone says or does as evidence that something is wrong with you or that you have done something wrong. In essence, you personalize the situation to prove that something is innately wrong about you. For example, your husband comes home edgy and irritable and does not give you much attention besides saying hello, and you immediately think, "He is mad at me; I must have done something wrong." Or your boss ignores an email for a few days and you think, "He must be planning to fire me."

COMMON DISTORTIONS IN THE WORRY TYPE
OF ALMOST ANXIETY

Black-and-white thinking: This is a classic type of anxiety- and depression-driven thought. It results from seeing only two possible alternatives for a situation, often polar opposite ends of the spectrum, without any gray area. Eduardo, for example, thought he was either having a heart attack and would die or he was going crazy. Someone else might think, "Either I do my job perfectly or I will get fired." In these cases, there is no middle-of-the-road, balanced alternative.

COMMON DISTORTIONS IN THE SOCIAL TYPE
OF ALMOST ANXIETY

Fortune telling and mind reading: Imagine that you are getting ready to give a presentation and you don't particularly like public speaking. As the day of the event approaches, you are likely to have many thoughts predicting what will happen during the talk (in other words, fortune telling). Because you are filtering these thoughts through a "crystal ball" that's every bit as questionable as the lenses of anxiety, you are likely to anticipate that the presentation, which is a situation you fear, will turn out in the worst way possible: "I won't be able to answer their questions well, so everyone in the audience will hate my presentation." Similarly, if you are planning to go on a first date next weekend, you might think, "He will notice that I am nervous, and he won't call me afterward." Fortune telling may lead you to avoid an anxiety-producing situation, which actually robs you of the opportunity to challenge the distorted thought.

Mind reading is a present-moment type of fortune telling. That is why both of these fall under the general umbrella of "jumping to conclusions." Let's go back to that first date. In fact, let's use an example of some mind reading I did on *my* most recent first date.

It was a rainy Sunday afternoon, and I was having coffee on a blind date with Bob, a friend of a friend. As I was explaining to him what I do for a living, he looked at me in an odd way, and I had an avalanche of mind-reading thoughts: "Here we go. He will make a joke about me being a psychologist and ask me if I can read his mind. Actually, maybe he thinks I am a nerd. Am I boring? Should I not be talking about work on a first date? What if he thinks that all I do is work?" These thoughts immediately made me a little anxious. Thankfully, I was able to catch these thoughts in real time and tell myself, "I have no data to support this. Maybe he is just curious about what I do. Perhaps he wasn't giving me a weird look—maybe that is just what he looks like when he is thinking."

As the conversation progressed, I learned that Bob is also an academic and enjoys discussing research studies! But even before I heard the real reason for his quizzical look, I had given myself an alternate explanation for Bob's "odd" expression that immediately decreased my anxiety and allowed me to re-engage in the conversation. You, too, will learn how to come up with more balanced thoughts in the next step.

COMMON DISTORTIONS IN THE PANIC TYPE
OF ALMOST ANXIETY

Catastrophizing: This occurs when you predict that an event will be awful and you will not be able to tolerate it. Patients say to me, "I will get so anxious during this family get-together that I will explode." Or "If she breaks up with me, I will never be able to get another girlfriend." Or "If I don't do well at this performance evaluation, I will never be able to move up into management." In Eduardo's case, he often worried about getting dizzy again and would think, "If I feel dizzy, I will faint and never regain consciousness." Generally speaking, when you catastrophize, you make any *small* event a *big* deal.

Probability overestimation: Another classic cognitive distortion in people with panic-like symptoms is to overestimate the chance of an event occurring. When I first talked to Eduardo and we discussed his symptoms, he told me that he was 80 percent certain that if he were to have another panic attack, he might "go crazy and lose my job."

As with all the other distortions, *you cannot use your anxiety as evidence when measuring probability*. For example, how likely is it that Bob won't want to go on another date with me? If I were gauging the probability at the moment when he gave me the "weird" look, then I might be 70 percent certain. However, if I gauge the likelihood based on *all* the first dates I have ever been on, then perhaps the probability would be different. If I calculated that probability, it would be very low, probably close to zero—especially given that he asked me out for a second date by the end of our first date!

Step 4: Take Your Thought to the Courtroom and Challenge It
Identifying and labeling your distorted, anxiety-driven thoughts are the first steps toward refocusing your anxiety lenses. However, those will not be enough. To be able to create alternative thoughts—thoughts based on reality and driven less by

anxiety—you have to learn how to challenge your thinking.

Again, I am not suggesting that you replace an *anxious* thought with a *happy* thought, but rather that you collect evidence to help you discover which line of thinking is more accurate. By challenging your thoughts, your anxiety will eventually start to decrease, and you naturally will start to have more balanced thinking.

By *evidence*, I mean anything that could be used in a court of law (as opposed to what couldn't be considered evidence: anxiety). When in doubt, ask yourself how a judge would respond to this evidence. To learn more about how to inspect your thoughts for evidence, let's look to Eduardo's thought that he was having a heart attack. Anytime that Eduardo felt his pulse increase even slightly, he jumped to the conclusion that *this time* he was having a heart attack. Even though several doctors reassured Eduardo that nothing was wrong with his heart, he had trouble believing it. As such, I asked Eduardo to evaluate his thought by asking two basic questions:

1. Do I have any evidence for this thought?

2. If no evidence exists, is there an alternate way to consider this thought? Even if this thought is true, is it helpful right now?

Figure 17 shows how Eduardo challenged his anxiety-fueled thinking with the help of these questions.

Figure 17.

How Eduardo Challenged His Anxiety-Fueled Thinking

STEP 1 FEELINGS	STEP 2 THOUGHTS	STEP 3 DISTORTIONS	STEP 4 EVIDENCE	RESPONSES
Anxious	I'm going to go crazy.	Catastrophizing	Do I have any evidence for this thought?	There is no evidence that feeling anxious equals going crazy.
Heart pounding	I will have a heart attack.	Fortune-telling	Is there an alternate way to consider this thought, if no evidence is possible?	I am likely to be anxious because I am thinking I will go crazy, but I don't have any evidence. In fact, I had the same feeling 100 times in the past month and I haven't had a heart attack.
Dizziness	I have a brain tumor.	Probability overestimation	Even if this thought is true, is it helpful right now?	Thinking that I am having a brain tumor is likely to be making me more anxious.

Following this example, for each thought you write down and label, ask yourself these two questions. Your goal is to broaden your thinking and arrive at more balanced, fact-based thinking with fewer anxiety-driven thoughts. Review Eduardo's example once again to see the steps that helped him to identify and challenge his thoughts. Then, work through these same steps in exercise 17 as you challenge your own anxiety-fueled thinking. You can also download this exercise at www.AlmostAnxious.com.

Eduardo's Outcome

Eduardo learned that most of his thoughts were driven by his almost anxiety rather than by facts. The responses that Eduardo came up with helped him to manage his almost anxiety and collect more balanced views of the world around him. In addition to working on changing his thoughts, Eduardo also agreed to stop seeking repeated reassurance from his wife and to start approaching social activities instead of avoiding them.

For most of the patients I work with, showing them how to cope with their thoughts is not enough, because they tend to avoid a *lot* of situations. After learning how to have more balanced thoughts, it's time to take those skills and stand up to your fears. In other words, it's time to *approach your lions*.

Exercise 17.

Challenging Your Anxiety-Fueled Thinking

STEP 1 FEELINGS	STEP 2 THOUGHTS	STEP 3 DISTORTIONS	STEP 4 EVIDENCE	RESPONSES
		☐ Emotional reasoning	Do I have any evidence for this thought?	
		☐ Personalizing	Is there an alternate way to consider this thought, if no evidence is possible?	
		☐ Black-and-white thinking		
		☐ Fortune telling	Even if this thought is true, is it helpful right now?	
		☐ Mind reading		
		☐ Catastrophizing		
		☐ Probability overestimation		

10

It's Time to Feel Comfortably Uncomfortable

Late one afternoon, my office phone rang. The caller had located me through my website and asked if I was taking new patients. The tone of her voice was strained, and her hesitation was palpable, almost as if there were something she wasn't telling me. I became intrigued as the conversation continued.

Mary's Story

Mary explained that she had found herself at a crossroad in her life. She wasn't "living up to her full potential," mostly because she was worrying a lot and not facing things that made her anxious. For example, Mary would have insightful ideas for improving the marketing department of the company she worked for, but instead of presenting them to her manager, she would share them with her co-workers and suggest that they take credit for them. Mary was concerned that her bosses might think that she and her ideas were "stupid."

Mary was single and had chosen to dedicate most of her time to her career as a mechanical engineer. She was good at what she did but "never excellent." Despite her social concerns and on-and-off worries, Mary lived a fulfilling life. She had a host of hobbies and friends, and she traveled the world. Yet here we were discussing her anxiety.

As we continued to talk, Mary told me about her childhood, which was difficult. A car accident left her father cognitively impaired and disabled, which in turn left most of the household responsibilities to Mary's mom, Susan. Her long hours at work and taking care of the home left her emotionally unavailable to Mary, who was an only child.

Mary said she believed that most of her current concerns and worries were related to her upbringing. She strongly felt that if Susan had been more emotionally available to her, she would not have her current "insecurities," as she called them.

The conversation came to a halt when I explained to Mary that I was a cognitive-behavioral therapist and that for us to work together, she would have to learn to slowly approach the things that she was fearful of, like taking more initiative at work.

I often explain to prospective patients that my goal is to teach them how to capitalize on their anxiety so they can live their lives "comfortably uncomfortable." What does that mean? At one end of the spectrum, the people who seek my professional help are stuck on the almost anxious hamster wheel, spending a lot of energy trying to get unstuck but feeling as though they are not getting any traction. In other words, they're uncomfortable.

At the other end, when people are completely comfortable,

they are relaxed and unproductive. Situated as they are at the very low end of the anxiety/performance curve, their lives are relaxed, but not as fulfilling as they could be. As the Yerkes-Dodson curve presented earlier in the book illustrated, you will be much more productive in the middle of the curve, as you face the enemy of avoidance (see figure 18).

Figure 18.
**Avoid or Approach? The "Quick Fix" versus
"Comfortably Uncomfortable" Dilemma**

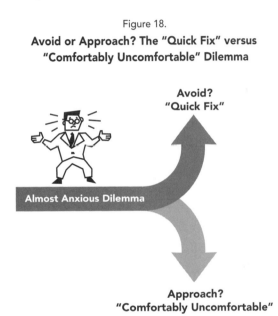

Let's get back to Mary's story. Mary was skeptical. She had already seen this quote on my website: "Life begins at the end of your comfort zone," by author Neale Donald Walsch. She strongly disagreed that exposure-based therapy—which requires approaching your fears by moving out of your comfort zone—would be helpful. It turned out that she'd already spent years in psychoanalysis, often seeing a therapist three to five times a week, and as a result was very reluctant to pursue cognitive-behavioral therapy for her almost anxiety. After all, if she could simply face what she was afraid of, she would not need to come to therapy, she said. Still, we arranged for her to come in for a visit.

In this chapter, I'll walk you through the general steps of exposure therapy, which are appropriate for all three almost anxious subtypes: worry, social, and physical. I'll use Mary's treatment progress, as well as the experience of other patients, to demonstrate how you can design your own exposure sessions to things that make you almost anxious.

Although the principles of exposure sound simple, my patients sometimes struggle with certain steps, so I'll trouble-shoot these areas where you, too, might get stuck. By learning these strategies, you can develop the mantra of "approach—not avoid—in a comfortably uncomfortable way."

Types of Exposure Therapy

Some definitions of the word exposure seem negative, like being exposed to harsh weather or being left out in the open where you're vulnerable to threats. But when you're managing your almost anxiety, exposure is a *good* thing.

Simply put, during exposure therapy, people face their fears by continuously and repeatedly approaching the things they are afraid of. It is one of the most studied types of treatment for anxiety disorders, and research has shown that exposure thera- py is an effective way to treat *all* the anxiety disorders discussed in this book. There's no reason to believe it won't work equally as well for almost anxiety.[1] That's why I use this method when treating patients who are almost anxious.

If a patient comes to me with almost anxiety involving dogs, I might have her start by looking at a picture of a dog, then looking at videos of dogs online. Over time, she'd progress to going into a room with a small dog, and perhaps she'd eventually be able to approach a big "scary" dog. The important element is to continue to *approach* the fearful situation.

There are three main types of exposure: in vivo, imaginal, and interoceptive exposure.

- **In vivo exposure:** This means exposure to actual situations, such as putting yourself next to a real dog, driving over bridges, or going skydiving. It requires more than just "being exposed" to a situation (having a chance encounter with a puppy at the Laundromat or struggling through a party doesn't count as exposure). You actually have to follow steps to ensure that your body learns that the feared situation is only a "false alarm." After all, if just being "exposed" to dogs would cure one's fear of dogs, I would have been out of a job a long time ago!

- **Imaginal exposure:** This is an alternative method when it is impossible or unsafe to conduct real-life exposure. For imaginal exposure, I would invite my patient to merely visualize the feared situation instead of approaching it in real life. For example, a patient with a fear of giving a presentation to a large audience might start by practicing imaginal exposure, given the logistical difficulties involved in assembling a roomful of people for a "practice" presentation. That being said, whenever possible, I strongly urge my patients to practice real-life in vivo exposure.

Exposure Goes High-Tech

Thanks to modern technology, a fourth kind of exposure, virtual reality exposure, is now available. People receiving this treatment are exposed to highly realistic, computer-generated simulations of feared situations or stimuli.

For example, one treatment that was developed for individuals with public speaking anxiety involved having them wear a headset that projected images of a full conference room or auditorium into their line of sight. The therapist could even control the reaction of the people in these virtual environments, having them yawn or applaud to tailor the exposure to the patient's needs.[2]

Virtual reality exposure has been used to treat many different kinds of anxiety, including specific phobias, social anxiety disorder, and panic disorder.[3] It may be useful as a stepping-stone for people with almost anxiety who are reluctant to jump right into in vivo exposure.

- **Interoceptive exposure:** This means exposing patients to their own bodily sensations, like the earlier example of Maggie (chapter 1), who spun around in a chair in my office to induce feelings of dizziness. Interoceptive exposure has been studied mostly for panic disorder, but clinicians often use it in addition to in vivo exposure for people who are particularly afraid of their own physical symptoms (like sweating or blushing).

People who are almost anxious can practice in vivo exposure on their own. However, if you think your panic-like symptoms fall in the severe range and you might benefit from interoceptive exposure, I would recommend that you seek the guidance of a professional who can ensure you're doing it properly.

One of the most difficult steps in interoceptive exposure is for people to tolerate their physiological symptoms. They are supposed to *stay* with the sensations, experiencing them and not running away from them. Theoretically, this is not different from in vivo or imaginal exposure, but because interoceptive exposure turns your limbic system (including your fight-or-flight response) to a very hot anxiety temperature, most people want to avoid it.

That is when having a trained professional comes in handy. This person can encourage you to stay with the situation and ensure that you are not using any avoidance methods. For example, often when I conduct interoceptive exposure therapy by asking patients to plug their nose with their fingers and breathe through a straw to limit the amount of oxygen they get, they will experience strong feelings of shortness of breath, dizziness, and sometimes even nausea. During the session, I have to coach them to stick with the situation and to ride the sensations out. After all, although their sensations are similar to what they would be in a truly dangerous situation—such as running from a lion—in this case the body is responding to the mere *thought* of danger; hence, it is just a false alarm.

It would also be fairly challenging for people to engage in imaginal exposure by themselves without the guidance of a trained professional. For example, on their own, people tend to not evoke a scenario that's "threatening" enough, and they often shut it off too early so they can escape it.

For those reasons, this chapter will focus on how to perform in vivo, or real-life, exposures on your own.

The Nuts and Bolts of In Vivo Exposure Therapy

Habituation—that is, getting accustomed to the anxiety-pro-voking situation—is the process by which exposure-based treatment works. Habituation through in vivo exposure calls on you to deliberately trigger your anxiety by exposing yourself to a fearful situation. By doing so, you learn to ride the anxiety out, knowing that it will naturally decrease as time passes. Although the focus of fear (heights, animals, social situations, and so on) is different for different types of almost anxiety, habituation happens regardless of the situation if you follow the principles highlighted next.

While you're practicing in vivo exposure, these three indi-cators will help you know if you're becoming habituated, or desensitized, to the situation that normally triggers your almost anxiety (see figure 19):

- Over time, the anxiety you feel *before* you expose your-self to the trigger (your baseline anxiety temperature) decreases.

- Over time, your anxiety doesn't peak as high as it did in earlier exposure sessions.

- Your anxiety doesn't stay at its peak level for as long as before either. The time that it takes for your anxiety to come down will become shorter with repeated real-life exposure.

Figure 19.

Avoidance versus Habituation

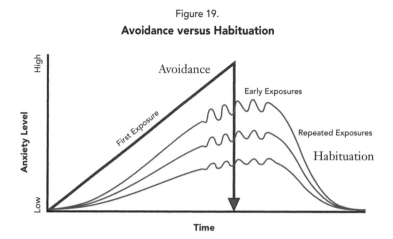

Repeatedly exposing yourself to your feared situation in this way requires being able to measure your "anxiety temperature." See chapter 6 for more on keeping an anxiety temperature. Figure 20 illustrates how such a thermometer works.

Figure 20.

Anxiety and Avoidance Thermometer

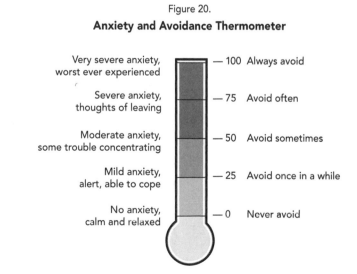

For example, let's consider my own anxiety temperature on my hike at Yosemite National Park, where I developed a temporary fear of heights. My baseline anxiety was around 40. From the beginning, I was a little nervous about the length of the hike since I hadn't trained much for it. When I started to fear that I might fall, my anxiety thermometer shot up to 70. If my friend had not been hiking with me, I might have avoided the rest of the hike altogether. But with a little help, I was able to complete it. By sticking to the hike, my anxiety temperature naturally dropped.

Once you have a measurement of your usual anxiety levels so you can track any changes, you can learn to practice in vivo exposure therapy using this six-step process:

1. Build a hierarchy.

2. Choose a practice situation, considering challenge and tolerance factors.

3. Stay in the situation until your peak anxiety decreases.

4. Repeat the same exposure right away (called *looping*).

5. Track your progress.

6. Reward yourself.

Step 1: Build a Hierarchy
This is a list of situations, people, or places that trigger your anxiety symptoms, with each item corresponding to a specific anxiety temperature. Your list should relate to your fears about one of your almost anxious areas, not a general list of fearful things. For example, in my fear hierarchy of heights, I would only list items that trigger my fear of heights—even if I am also

afraid of snakes while hiking, this issue would not go on that list.

I suggest to patients that their hierarchy should range from 0 to 100, with 0 being no anxiety and 100 being the worst anxiety they have ever experienced. Exercise 18 is a blank hierarchy list that you can use to start thinking about your own patterns. You can also download this exercise at www.AlmostAnxious .com. If you have symptoms of all three almost anxious subtypes, create a hierarchy for each subtype.

Figure 21 shows what Mary's anxiety hierarchy might look like.

Figure 21.
Mary's Anxiety Hierarchy

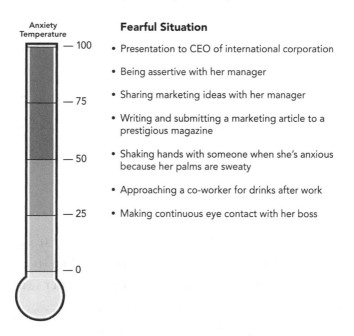

Anxiety Temperature	Fearful Situation
— 100	• Presentation to CEO of international corporation
	• Being assertive with her manager
— 75	• Sharing marketing ideas with her manager
	• Writing and submitting a marketing article to a prestigious magazine
— 50	• Shaking hands with someone when she's anxious because her palms are sweaty
	• Approaching a co-worker for drinks after work
— 25	• Making continuous eye contact with her boss
— 0	

As you build your hierarchy, omit items that make you anxious but that you don't necessarily avoid, as well as items that don't cause any significant interference or distress in your life. For example, Mary was afraid of sharks, but she did not avoid going to the beach. In her first attempt at making a hierarchy, she rated swimming with sharks as 100. Given that I was not treating her for shark phobia and she had no strong aspirations to go scuba diving, we removed that item from her hierarchy. So the lesson here is to stay with items that are specific to your anxiety symptoms. They should also be situations that you can approach repeatedly and use to measure your progress.

At first, you may only be able to think of items that you find very difficult to face, and so your hierarchy only includes high-anxiety items. However, this kind of list will ensure you remain stuck. As I tell my patients, if you were able to start by facing something that makes you 100 percent anxious, you would have done so already! Instead, you'll need to start with something smaller that makes you "comfortably uncomfortable" and then gradually progress into more fearful situations. One way to overcome this problem is to break one major item in your hierarchy into several smaller items. Cristina, who was afraid of driving over bridges, can show you how.

Cristina's Story

Cristina was a successful saleswoman in her mid-fifties who did most of her sales calls from her office. For years she rarely had to drive around Boston, which has several bridges that particularly bothered her—especially the high, ten-lane Zakim Bridge over the Charles River. However, as the economy changed, Cristina's job description started to broaden. She was required to start visiting some of her clients at their sites, which, to her dismay, were often on the other side of bridges.

Cristina was almost anxious around bridges to the extent that she would avoid them when possible, but she would face them for her job. However, by the time she crossed a bridge and arrived at a client's site for a sales meeting, she would be tired and already dreading the trip home.

Since the only item on Cristina's hierarchy was driving over bridges, we had to break it down into smaller fears. Cristina had less difficulty driving over some of the shorter bridges in town like the Harvard Bridge, which rated a 50 on her anxiety temperature scale. But she got stuck when it came to the highest anxiety-producing item in her hierarchy: the Zakim Bridge. So we set up her hierarchy as shown in figure 22.

Figure 22.
Cristina's Anxiety Hierarchy

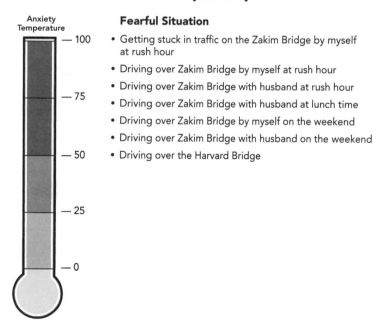

Anxiety
Temperature

Fearful Situation

— 100 • Getting stuck in traffic on the Zakim Bridge by myself at rush hour

• Driving over Zakim Bridge by myself at rush hour

• Driving over Zakim Bridge with husband at rush hour

— 75 • Driving over Zakim Bridge with husband at lunch time

• Driving over Zakim Bridge by myself on the weekend

• Driving over Zakim Bridge with husband on the weekend

— 50 • Driving over the Harvard Bridge

— 25

— 0

With the knowledge of her anxiety hierarchy, we were able to start practicing exposures to the bridge at a level that she could tolerate while feeling comfortably uncomfortable.

Using figure 22 as a model, build your own anxiety hierarchy next, using exercise 18; you can also download this exercise at www.AlmostAnxious.com. In step 2, you'll learn how to choose the right level of exposure.

Exercise 18.

Building My Own Anxiety Hierarchy

Anxiety Temperature	Fearful Situation

— 100

— 75

— 50

— 25

— 0

Step 2: Choose a Practice Situation, Considering Challenge and Tolerance Factors

Once you have built your hierarchy, the next step is to select the anxiety-triggering situation for practicing in vivo exposure. Most of my patients wonder which situation they should choose.

Cristina did not start by going to what she considered the scariest bridge in Boston. Instead, she started by driving back and forth over the Harvard Bridge, a flat bridge without much traffic, during the middle of the morning. Cristina rated her anxiety temperature at 50 for that bridge, which is why she started with it. How did we decide on this level? We based our decision on the challenge and tolerance factors, which together would lead Cristina to feel "comfortably uncomfortable."

- *Challenge factor:* Pick an item in your hierarchy that will challenge you sufficiently. Usually I recommend something that generates an anxiety level between 40 and 60. If you are not experiencing any anxiety, then you are not practicing in vivo exposure. You need to be out of your comfort zone enough to trigger the exposure.

- *Tolerance factor:* Your tolerance factor refers to your ability to stay in the situation long enough for habituation to occur. If you choose an appropriate challenge factor, you will be *comfortably uncomfortable*, but you won't feel the need to run out of the situation. Remember that for habituation to happen, you must expose yourself to a situation, then do the opposite of what you have been doing—meaning you are to *approach, not avoid* the situation.

To determine your tolerance factor, it is important to recognize where your overall anxiety temperature is right before you start an exposure practice—namely, what is your *baseline anxiety?* Many things affect people's anxiety temperature, such as sleep deprivation, hunger, chronic life stressors, and family illness.

Assume, for example, that we had agreed Cristina would practice "driving over Zakim Bridge with her husband on the weekends," which she had ranked as a 50 on her hierarchy. In other words, Cristina believed that her peak anxiety on this bridge could reach a value of 50 under these conditions.

However, suppose that Cristina and her husband had a brief disagreement about parenting right before leaving to practice her exposure. I suspect Cristina would start to feel more discomfort and anxiety, which could lead to a higher anxiety temperature as she drove over this bridge.

What should Cristina have done if this happened? One way to manage heightened baseline anxiety levels before exposure is to do things that help you cool off. In Cristina's case, that might have involved going for a walk before practicing exposure or even delaying the drive until she was able to resolve her conflict with her husband. What Cristina should *not* do if her baseline anxiety spiked before her exposure practice is to avoid carrying out the exposure. In such a situation, I would have encouraged her to find ways to lower her baseline anxiety or to practice something lower in her hierarchy, but I would have strongly discouraged her from avoiding the session. After all, that only teaches her what she already believes: "I can't drive over bridges."

If you have trouble with your first exposure practice, consider turning to your social support network. Just as Cristina brought her husband along for her first trek across the bridge that she found most fearful, you can bring someone too. Yes, eventually you want to face your fears by yourself, but there is nothing wrong with getting some help in the beginning. After all, don't personal trainers help get us started in our exercise practice? This is no different.

Step 3: Stay in the Situation until Your Peak Anxiety Decreases

As you probably know from experience, once you approach something that you are afraid of, your anxiety thermometer will rise, often suddenly.

In Mary's case, when she tried to maintain eye contact with her boss during a meeting, she quickly learned that her peak anxiety was a little higher than the 25 she predicted (in fact, it quickly rose to 40). Once you reach your peak, you will naturally want to do anything to get out of the situation (in other words, to avoid). But the trick is to stay with it long enough for your peak anxiety to fall by *half.* For Mary, that meant she would have to keep talking to her boss, asking more questions and making eye contact, until her overall anxiety level fell to 20.

Staying in the situation until the peak anxiety comes down by half is hard for most of my patients. Cristina would experience her peak anxiety midway through the Harvard Bridge, but as she saw the bridge coming to an end, she would start to feel better. Had Cristina's peak anxiety decreased by 50 percent or was she just experiencing relief because the session was over? There was only one way to test this: by driving over the bridge again, right away. If Cristina's anxiety midway through the bridge peaked as high as it did the first time, then I would conclude that she had not experienced habituation yet.

That brings us to our next step.

Step 4: Repeat the Same Exposure Right Away

The urge to avoid is a powerful enemy that you're going to have to fight during your exposure sessions. For habituation to occur, you must "loop" your exposure practices. "Looping" basically means that you go right back into the situation. By looping, you learn that what you are experiencing is a "false alarm" and not "real danger."

The concept of looping is a point at which many of my patients get stuck for a few reasons. First, most people have an immediate sense of relief once they have faced their fear. For example, Cristina felt better as she approached the end of the bridge. But that was not habituation; rather, it was relief that she was "done." Looping ensures that habituation occurs. For Cristina, looping required turning around and driving right back over the bridge. For Mary, it meant that she would walk back into her boss's office and find a reason to ask him more questions or to seek clarification about the project they were working on so she could make eye contact with him again.

Through looping, your preexposure anxiety and peak anxiety start to decrease, and overcoming your fear becomes a habit. Each exposure session should involve practicing the same item at least three times (or three loops). Cristina would drive over the Harvard Bridge many times, back and forth, until her peak anxiety came down by half. That would be one exposure session, or one loop.

Here's a summary of what looping exposures involve:

* approaching the situation and doing it over and over again until habituation occurs (the peak falls by 50 percent)

- going right back into the situation and practicing again
- doing the same procedure at least three times (three loops)

One of the challenges my patients face is fitting these exposures into their busy schedules, which often means they try to do exposure sessions while also getting other things done. For example, Cristina thought she could just change her route to work to include the Harvard Bridge and it would count as an "exposure session." Although she was certainly "exposing" herself to driving over the bridge, she was *not* practicing exposure therapy because she wasn't looping through the situation enough times for her peak anxiety to come down by half.

So make sure to set aside plenty of time for your exposure sessions. I suggest at least forty-five minutes daily at the outset. As you learn to do this, you might be able to practice less frequently. Keep in mind that exposure work is much like exercising. The more often you go to the gym, the stronger you get. The more you practice exposure, the lower your anxiety will climb. Eventually you will overcome your fear—but practice is key!

Step 5: Track Your Progress

During an exercise program, some people keep a log of their workouts, recording data like how much they lifted or how fast they ran. This is also helpful during your exposure "exercise" program. Only by keeping records of your sessions will you be able to see how well they are working and to troubleshoot problem areas. Additionally, by taking notes on your exposure sessions, you will know when you are no longer getting anxious in a certain situation, and you will be able to move on to another item in your hierarchy. I would recommend reproducing the form in exercise 19 and using it daily to keep track of your exposures. You can also download this form at www.Almost Anxious.com.

Exercise 19.

Tracking My In Vivo Exposures

TIME	ANXIETY LEVEL

Step 6: Reward Yourself

My patients often forget to pat themselves on the back for the hard work they are doing. They tend to focus more on their "failed exposures" than on the times they were able to "drive over" their personal version of the scary bridge. However, in my book, there are no failed exposures. I firmly believe that as long as you are practicing and abiding by the principles in this chapter, you are succeeding. Some exposures will be more difficult than others, and at times you will avoid situations because your anxiety temperature rises too high too fast. As long as you return to the anxiety-provoking situation and try again, you are succeeding in fighting your avoidance!

For that reason, I think it is very important to recognize the small victories and celebrate them and to find ways to reward yourself as you continue approaching your feared situations, places, or things. Mary wrote a list of rewards she could choose from every time she completed an exposure session. She included things like these:

- taking time from work to go for a leisurely walk

- getting a manicure

- taking a bubble bath

Although most of these rewards were small, they still worked to remind Mary that she had faced the enemy—avoidance—and had succeeded despite her almost anxiety. I would urge you to create your own list of rewards you find meaningful, from small tokens for your beginning and intermediate steps to a larger reward when you complete your exposure to the item at the top of your hierarchy. Cristina scheduled a trip to Florida with her husband after she worked up to overcoming her fear of driving over the Zakim Bridge. For an extra challenge, they decided to vacation in the St. Petersburg area so she could drive over the Sunshine Skyway Bridge, which is more than four miles long. I am delighted to report that Cristina was able to drive over the bridge not once but three times, just to practice looping!

Common Obstacles to Exposure

One reason some people don't experience a decrease in peak anxiety over time when practicing real-life exposure is that they're still engaging in avoidance, often in a subtle way. Here are some issues to watch for that can be considered avoidance:

Medications. Some people with anxiety are prescribed benzodiazepines, a class of anxiety medications that are fast acting—they make you feel better almost immediately. Examples include Xanax, Valium, Klonopin, and Ativan. Data suggest that benzodiazepines can interfere with the exposure process, especially if taken right before or after an exposure session.[4]

This makes sense, given that the purpose of exposure is to learn to face the anxiety and not control or change it. By taking a fast-acting medication, you would actually be doing the opposite. If you are taking any medication from this class, talk with your doctor before trying exposure therapy.

Some people's baseline anxiety temperature is so elevated that they might benefit from taking one of these medications for the short term. When my patients are considering this approach, I often talk to their prescribing doctor to ensure that the medication is not acting as a crutch during our exposure sessions but is only being used to help them manage their overall anxiety level day to day. This usually means that the doctor will prescribe this medication on a regular schedule instead of an "as needed" approach, which helps the patient separate the effects of a lower overall baseline anxiety from what we are doing in exposure therapy.

Relaxation. Although relaxation practices such as progressive muscle relaxation, meditation, and breathing retraining can be helpful as supplemental ways to bring down your day-to-day anxiety, they can also be subtle ways for people to avoid exposure.

For example, when Cristina first started driving over bridges, she would try to relax by slowing down her breathing. This may sound like a healthy approach, but it allowed her to avoid fully experiencing the anxiety related to her fear of driving over bridges.

Cristina instead learned to "ride the wave of anxiety" and just allow it to exist, without trying to control it by breathing more slowly. You may be thinking, "But that would just make me more anxious." And you are right: this does momentarily increase your anxiety, but over time it starts to decrease. So, if you are going to practice relaxation, just make sure it is not before or immediately after an exposure session.

Self-talk. Another subtle way people might avoid exposure is by minimizing the experience as they're practicing it. For example, Mary was particularly fearful of rejection when asking her co-workers out for drinks. So as she was about to do it, she would say to herself, "It's okay if they say no—this is only to practice exposure. It isn't real." By discounting the practice in her mind, she immediately felt better, which I helped her recognize as a type of avoidance. Mary decided to up the ante and invite the *entire* office out for happy hour, thus increasing her anxiety thermometer and fighting back against the avoidance.

CONTINUED ON NEXT PAGE

CONTINUED FROM PREVIOUS PAGE

Subtle avoidance. I haven't yet treated a patient who didn't engage in *some* type of subtle avoidance. You can think of subtle avoidance as steps that would make your anxiety go down slightly. As noted earlier, researchers call these *safety behaviors*, and they also interfere with exposure therapy. In fact, successfully reducing safety behaviors is predictive of long-term treatment success.[5] Here are a few common ones:

- answering a question with a question to avoid engaging in personal conversation
- always carrying anxiety medication in case of a panic attack
- avoiding activities that could lead to panic-like sensations, such as drinking caffeine, exercising, or engaging in sexual activity

If you are engaging in any obvious avoidance or subtle avoidance, be sure to address it while you're practicing exposure exercises.

With all that we've discussed in mind, let's return to Mary, whom we met at the beginning of this chapter.

Mary's Outcome

Mary and I worked together for six months after our initial phone conversation. At first, she was very skeptical of using a cognitive-behavioral approach to tackle her almost anxiety. She was especially apprehensive of trying in vivo exposure.

Mary would find all sorts of reasons why she could not be more assertive about voicing her ideas in the workplace or setting up social functions with her co-workers. But slowly, she started to come around.

I knew Mary would get better the day she arrived at my office and said she had bought a refrigerator magnet—actually, one for herself and one for me—that read "Life begins at the end of your comfort zone." After many months of working together, Mary explained that she finally understood that if she just kept approaching slowly, her worst fears would not come true and she would eventually get more comfortable in the situations she feared. By the end of our treatment, Mary was regularly contributing ideas to her boss on how to improve processes in her workplace.

I still have her magnet on my refrigerator door to remind me not only of my work with Mary but also of how powerful exposure-based therapy can be in treating avoidance and giving people their lives back. Using the tools in this chapter, you too can reclaim your life.

I'd like to shift gears a bit now and talk about an approach that can help you stay present in the current moment while riding the anxiety wave. It's called "mindfulness."

❖

| 11 |

Be Here Now

*You must live in the present, launch yourself on every wave,
find your eternity in each moment.*

— HENRY DAVID THOREAU

"Mindfulness" is a simple concept that generates a variety of impressions among my patients. Some take to it immediately. Some struggle with it until it feels natural. Others give it a try and lose interest before they reap its benefit.

A good definition of mindfulness is "the experience of paying attention, in the present moment, non-judgmentally."[1] In the past decade, mindfulness-based therapies have received a lot of attention for treating anxiety and depression, as well as physical health problems.

When you're mindful, you're not mourning the past. You're not fearing the future. You're not generating scenes of catastrophe that could strike you. That's because none of these anxiety-producing worlds really exist! Instead, your mind is attuned to the sights, sounds, and sensations around you right here, right now. When your mind starts to drift, you gently allow it to recenter on the present moment. That's mindfulness in its simplest form. But attaining it isn't so simple.

Mindfulness is a way to stay anchored in the present moment, which many people have trouble doing in this modern world. An inability to stay present isn't surprising, given the increased demands on people's time, combined with a common desire to stay connected with others via email, cell phones, and social media. People feel pressured to always stay "on," plugged into a virtual world that keeps sending them input and requires their constant attention.

You and I are encouraged to do more things faster, and all at the same time. The resulting overload can leave you feeling like you have been hit by a tsunami, one that flings you into the past (stewing over the opportunities that you didn't take), into the future (worrying about threats and challenges that haven't arrived yet), or into dozens of other people's lives (via Facebook status updates and Twitter feeds). All of these scenarios completely rob you of the gift of the present moment.

When you aren't living in the moment, you're not performing at your optimal level. In one study, researchers compared reading comprehension between participants who were and were not instant messaging while reading a passage. The researchers found that while participants in both groups performed equally well on a reading comprehension test, those in the instant messaging group took significantly longer to read the passage (not counting the time that they were messaging).[2] These results suggest that distracted, divided attention comes at a cost.

In this chapter, I'll offer ways to practice mindfulness based on my research and clinical experiences, as well as my own efforts to become more mindful over the past decade. Much like many of the skills in your anxiety tool kit, mindfulness takes practice, patience, and self-compassion. It also requires you to keep reasonable outcomes in mind. If your goal from mindfulness is to always be calm and to not experience any anxiety, then you will likely become frustrated while trying to practice it. However, mindfulness might be an excellent practice for you if your goal is to

- be more present in your own life.
- become an observer of your experiences.
- live with your thoughts in the current moment instead of the past or future.

When I first met Gretchen, a patient who discovered the benefits of mindfulness, she arrived in my office as a perfect example of someone struggling with almost anxiety.

Gretchen's Story

To a casual acquaintance, Gretchen might have appeared to have her life under control. She's an architect and mother of two, married to a caring stay-at-home dad, Morris. Indeed, her world contained many wonderful elements. She enjoyed her kids, ages ten and twelve, and her relationship with Morris was rewarding. She did have long days because of her commute into the city from her Boston suburb, but she saw the train ride as a chance to catch up on work so she would have less to do at home.

As their children grew older, Morris, an accountant by training, started doing consulting work during tax season, which boosted the household's finances and provided funds for a nice family trip every year.

Gretchen was able to find time for the kind of hobbies and social interactions that are important for keeping anxiety in check. And she tried to eat healthy and exercise a few times a week. Still, Gretchen had recently noticed that she had more trouble relaxing, and she was feeling a little more nervous than usual. After she attended a yoga retreat, she found that she had significant trouble stopping her worries, which prompted her to come see me.

Her girlfriends had planned the weeklong yoga meditation getaway, and Gretchen signed on even though she wasn't particularly interested in either yoga or mediation. She figured she could always bail out early if it wasn't grabbing her and until then, she'd just enjoy her time with friends.

Gretchen said the retreat was difficult at first. She had trouble slowing down her thinking, and her mind kept drifting off, planning other things to do between the sessions. She really wanted to quit meditating and just enjoy her downtime, but her friends urged her to stick with it. By the end of the week, she did notice that she was more relaxed and less tense. But something strange also happened: once she came home, she noticed that she had more trouble "stopping or controlling my worries." In the weeks to come, Gretchen continued to be edgy and worried. She was having particular trouble enjoying leisure time with her family. When they were relaxing together with a movie at home on a Saturday night, her mind would wander, making lists of things she had to do the next week, which would cause her to grow irritable. Even her kids commented that Gretchen was more tightly wound than usual.

At our first appointment, I asked Gretchen to complete the GAD-7 tool, which measures overall levels of anxiety (the same assessment you completed in chapter 1). She had a total score of 8, which falls within the almost anxious spectrum. You might predict that Gretchen would score high on item 2, "not being able to stop or control worrying," which is correct. She rated that as a 3, indicating she experienced it nearly every day.

Gretchen's difficulty controlling her anxiety and worries weren't quite at a clinical level, but they were interfering with her happiness.

She had noticed the value of mindfulness meditation at her retreat and heard that I had some expertise in it, so she thought I could help her continue it. Still, she was a little ambivalent about establishing a mindfulness practice. Although she had found it helpful in decreasing some of her worry symptoms, she was also puzzled that they'd become uncontrollable after the retreat. As a result, she was not sure of its potential benefits. Why invest time in a practice that might just make her worry more?

Gretchen also wondered how she could integrate mindfulness into her busy life. At the retreat, it seemed easy. There she had no emails, no distractions, and no husband or children underfoot. Finally, Gretchen's goals for therapy were not to do more yoga or become more mindful. She simply wanted to live a fuller, more content, less worried life. Would mindfulness actually help her with that?

Gretchen became more receptive to the idea when she and I reviewed some of the literature on mindfulness together. Although she was an architect, her father was a neuroscientist, and her family had always discussed how different factors can transform the brain and mind. As a result, Gretchen was particularly intrigued by the studies that found structural and functional changes in the brain after mindfulness practice.

These findings finally convinced her to accept the value of mindfulness. Her exact words were, "The question is not why practice mindfulness. The question is, given these results, why *not* practice mindfulness?"

Mindfulness Produces Results

Therapists have found a place for mindfulness while treating many physical and emotional concerns, including these:[3]

- depression
- generalized anxiety disorder
- eating disorders
- psychological distress in cancer patients
- physical pain

In a recent study that compiled the results of thirty-nine earlier studies, researchers concluded that a mindfulness-based approach was quite effective for decreasing symptoms of depression and anxiety.[4] One point that makes this especially relevant to people with almost anxiety is that not all of the participants in these studies had full-fledged anxiety or depressive disorder.

Mindfulness and the Brain

Studies have shown that mindfulness practice actually changes functions in the brain and body. For example, in one study, researchers used electroencephalography (EEG) to measure electrical activity in the brains of people who were and weren't practicing mindfulness meditation. Participants in the mindful-ness group had more activity in an area of the brain associated with positive mood.[5] In the same study, researchers document-ed that people who practiced mindfulness meditation had an increased antibody response to the flu vaccine. This finding further supports the benefits of mindfulness meditation in overall physical health.

Another study demonstrated that mindfulness training may change the connections within the brain. Researchers con-ducted functional magnetic resonance imaging (fMRI) scans on people who had completed eight weeks of mindfulness training and on people who had not. The brain scans revealed increased connections within auditory and visual networks in the brains of those who had completed the training. Furthermore, they had lower rates of simultaneous activation in auditory and visual brain regions. These findings suggest that mindfulness training may improve the brain connections involved in sen-sory processing, as well as the brain's ability to focus specifically on auditory or visual information.[6]

Further research, which involved MRI scans of people's brains before and after mindfulness-based stress reduction training, indicated an increase in gray-matter density in sev-eral important brain regions related to memory, learning, and emotional processing. This suggests that mindfulness training could increase brain concentration in these crucial areas.[7]

All of these studies indicate that mindfulness is a tool you can use to change the very function and structure of your brain to foster a fuller, more enjoyable life with less anxiety.

How Can I Practice Mindfulness?

Many of my patients have experiences similar to what Gretchen went through at the yoga retreat: they find the concept of mindfulness easier to apply in a special supportive environment, but much more challenging to fit into their routines once they're back at home.

One way to begin a mindfulness practice is to bring what meditators call a "beginner's mind." In essence, you are encouraged to always practice meditation or other mindfulness-based activities, like yoga, as if you were encountering it for the first time.

I finally understood "beginner's mind" when one of my friends recently emailed me a video of her nearly two-year-old son, Eric, playing with an ice cube for the first time. His fascination with the cold object was profound. Every time he felt the intense cold of the ice, he would drop it. Then he'd giggle and crawl toward the melting cube as it slid away from him. He would grab it again, and again it would slip out of his chubby toddler hands. This "beginner's mind" practice repeated itself over and over until the ice cube finally melted away.

Eric's approach to the ice cube is what I would encourage you to bring to your mindfulness practice. Curiosity, compassion, patience, and a beginner's mind will serve you well as you learn to center yourself in the present moment.

With that spirit in mind, I encourage you to model your approach on the steps that Gretchen took for practicing mindfulness.

Think Small

Gretchen needed to restructure her schedule to carve out time for regular practice. To that end, she and I worked on setting small and realistic goals. I'd recommend that you do the same. *How* you choose to be mindful is less important than your ability to follow through with your practice.

When people think about changing their behavior, they often have big, lofty goals, like meditating for an hour or doing yoga daily. Although both would be great for you, they are most likely unrealistic demands on your time. Instead, committing to small, steady, focused practice sessions is the way to go.

Commit with Creativity

Your ability to learn any new skill relies on your commitment to it. I realized this a few years ago when I noticed that I had invested a lot of energy into many aspects of my life, but I had only partially committed to mindfulness. You have likely found yourself in a similar position, when daily demands distract you from the "good for you" elements like exercising, eating healthy, or relaxing, and you tell yourself, "This will be temporary until I get through this busy period." Yet time moves on, and when you bring your attention back to the present moment, you find that you're struggling a little more.

You can practice mindfulness in a million different ways. It merely requires that you bring your attention back to the present moment in a nonjudgmental way. For some people, running focuses their mind on the current moment as their feet strike the ground and their breath moves in and out. Gretchen didn't have this anymore (she had been an avid runner, but an injury limited her mileage), so she had to find a different way to practice.

I asked Gretchen to examine her life and try to identify areas where she could create small gaps in her schedule for implementing a mindfulness practice that would not disrupt her entire life. Her list included these possibilities:

- staying in her car to focus on her breath for five minutes after parking
- brushing her teeth in the morning with an awareness of being in the present moment
- parking a few blocks away from her destination so she could walk mindfully
- checking her email only three times daily and not doing any other activities while answering emails
- engaging mindfully with her family for small periods of time, such as during a family meal at least once a week with a ban on TV, phone calls, and other distractions

As you might have noticed, some of the items on Gretchen's list relied on her family for social support. Much like when you're exercising, eating healthy, or changing your thinking, social support can be vital when working on mindfulness. I would encourage you, whenever possible, to recruit your support system to help you focus on the here and now.

Also like Gretchen, ask yourself, "Where in my life can I find at least five minutes to practice mindfulness each day?" and write down your answers on a sheet of paper. Then put your plan into practice.

Find Mindful Rhythms and Images

Have you ever eaten half a jar of peanut butter or a pint of ice cream without really tasting it? Have you ever driven down a familiar street with your mind wandering and realized that you don't remember the last mile?

Many people go through much of their lives in that type

of blur, not noticing, tasting, seeing, smelling, and feeling the things they've been encountering. That's because they're dwelling on the past, fearing the future, or spending time in a daydream world instead. And they're missing delightful gifts that the present moment is giving them in the real world.

Being mindful means noticing these things. Here are a few sensations and objects you regularly encounter that you can use to set yourself into the present moment.

Mindfulness of the Breath

When starting to practice mindfulness, it's helpful to have a point of reference for focusing your attention. When your mind drifts, you bring your attention back to that same point over and over without scolding yourself for wandering.

A common reference point that mindfulness teachers suggest is your breath. Bring your attention to your nose, and be aware of your breath passing in and out, in and out. When your mind wanders, refocus on your breath. Guide your attention back to your breath, much like Eric did with his ice cube.

"I can't hold my attention on my breath. My mind wanders and starts to make lists!" you might say. You're not alone. As mentioned earlier, mindfulness teacher Jon Kabat-Zinn often describes our minds as monkeys jumping from tree to tree. They're seldom focused on a single point.

But the goal of mindfulness practice isn't to *arrive* anywhere. You're not failing because your mind is wandering away from your breath. The exercise is not even about holding your attention on your breath: it's about observing what happens when you pause long enough to notice your breath.

Given how difficult it is for us to slow down our minds, I'd recommend starting with just a minute or two at a time.

Remember, the goal is to practice, not to reach a destination!

Mindful Walking

If being mindful of your breath proves to be too difficult, then try something *physical*. I started my mindfulness journey by practicing mindful walking. For a set period of time, I slow down my pace, turn off my phone, and allow myself to use all five senses to observe the process of walking. I ask myself these questions:

- How do my feet feel against the concrete?
- How does my body feel in the present moment?
- What's in my surroundings?

Given that I am human, I often struggle at the start of a session as my "judgmental mind" kicks into full gear and starts telling me "I feel stiff," "I'm tired," "I should be returning my patients' messages." So I can tell you that the avalanche of thoughts *always* comes. But I don't fight them. I just welcome the thoughts, often telling myself something like, "My mind is alive and feisty today!" I allow the thoughts to pass, and then I turn my attention back to the sensations related to my mindful walk.

Mindfulness of Sounds

In his book *Peace Is Every Step: The Path of Mindfulness in Everyday Life*, Vietnamese Zen master Thich Nhat Hanh wrote an excellent passage on "mindful bells." He suggests that one should take a few moments to be mindful whenever the telephone rings. Observe the sound of the ring or ringtone. Allow yourself to breathe and focus on the present moment before answering.

I like this visualization of mindfulness, but in recent years I've noticed that my phone rings less and text messages buzz a lot more. So borrowing from the master, I have tried to practice "mindful text messaging," in which I invite myself to take three deep breaths before reading the message and another three breaths before responding to it. I can't tell you how hard this practice has been, given that I often answer my texts on automatic pilot. Yet I find more connection with the present moment when I am able to mindfully text.

Where in your life can you adapt this concept? Could you practice mindfulness when your email inbox beeps? How about when you hear a car pass outside your home? Work to find something small you can commit to that creates a bit of space for the present moment in the chaos of the storm of modern-day life.

Mindful Visualization

Imagery is another powerful way to practice mindfulness, especially if you are a visual person. The literature on mindfulness meditation describes many ways you can stay present using visualization. I'll describe two methods that I often use in my clinical practice, but I encourage you to try others until you find the one that suits you best.

- **Leaves.** Think of your thoughts as leaves on a river. Allow the thoughts to exist without attaching to them, without trying to change them, and without fighting them. In my mind's eye, I try to think of big, colorful fall leaves floating on a calm river. I often find that the river of my mind looks more like class-5 white water. Still, while I'm observing it, I try to let my thoughts float freely. That is the mindful-watching approach!

• **Clouds.** Envision your thoughts as clouds floating through the sky. Set aside some time without interruption to observe your thoughts passing by like clouds in the sky on a sunny day. You will quickly notice that you enjoy the thoughts that are pleasant and likely want the ones that are upsetting to blow on past. Try to observe both the white clouds and the stormy ones without judgment.

Whichever visualization style you follow, practice as often as possible. I would recommend trying different types. Some will feel easier than others. One caveat is that learning a skill takes time, and this includes mindfulness. So try to stick to one style at a time (such as the river or the clouds) to give it a fair shot before turning your attention to another type.

> **Suggestions for a Daily Mindfulness Practice**
>
> Here are some mindfulness practices to consider trying:
>
> • mindfulness breathing
>
> • mindfulness walking
>
> • mindfulness sounds (bells, phone, text messages, email alerts)
>
> • imagery (river, clouds, ocean waves)

Troubleshoot Your Mindfulness Practice

Once you have established an attitude of mindfulness, be aware that you are likely to hit bumps along your journey. There are three main challenges that, like my patients, you might face.

Anchoring in the Present Moment

Most of my patients have trouble staying present in the moment. That is especially true for those who are battling worries, since their minds are usually in the past ("What did I do wrong?") and in the future ("How is this going to turn out?").

One of the visualizations I share with my patients that many find helpful for staying in the present moment is *anchoring their boats*. When life grows more stressful and you are feeling worried, visualize a *Titanic*-size anchor being dropped deep in the ocean as your personal steadying point. It's not pulling you under but rather is keeping you from being swept away. Picturing a stable anchor tends to hold me steady, no matter how choppy the ocean of my life gets.

Gretchen found it helpful to "anchor" before she headed into a particularly stressful situation. For example, before her monthly staff meeting, she used to continually worry that her bosses would say that she wasn't doing enough work or that she would have to take on more time-intensive projects. Then she started taking a five-minute mindful walk on the way to those meetings, visualizing herself dropping her anchor into the ocean, where it kept her "boat" stable in the present moment.

The Desire to "Train Your Puppy" in One Day

During a recent yoga retreat to the Kripalu Center in western Massachusetts, I got a massage from a thoughtful young man named Nathan. We were discussing many of the difficulties that come with cultivating mindfulness, covering many of the issues I've discussed in this chapter. Nathan provided me with a beautiful metaphor that I would like to share with you.

Often Nathan's students tell him that they are unable to meditate, having tried and failed at it. When Nathan asks about their attempts, many report that they've usually tried it only a few times, giving up in frustration over their "monkey minds." Nathan's response is always the same: "What if you were just bringing a new puppy home? Would you expect him to be potty trained on the first day? Of course not! That would be unrealistic."

The same is true for mindfulness. In some ways, training your mind to be present is no different from training your puppy. Gretchen struggled with this concept. After all, she was a skilled architect with a meticulous mind, not a puppy. She felt that if she just tried harder, she could become more mindful faster. But it's impossible to rush mindfulness. Eventually, Gretchen found that what helped her was to set small goals and reward herself for practicing, but not to focus on outcomes.

Dealing with Your Own Times Square

Another frequent challenge to mindfulness is people's environment. A patient of mine, who recently moved from New York City to Boston, commented that she had found it impossible to be mindful while living in New York's constant stimulation. I agreed with her that it is challenging to practice when literally millions of people are surrounding you, lights are flashing in your eyes, and your city never sleeps. But it's not impossible. You just have to take yourself out of this environment for a brief time. In her case, I asked if she ever strolled through Central Park—a calm green oasis amid the maelstrom of Manhattan—on a mindful walk.

Even if you can't find a quiet place, you can still center

yourself in the moment. I recently attempted this by practicing mindful walking through Times Square while visiting a friend in New York. It was indeed challenging to stay present in the moment while being bumped by people and hearing a din of jackhammers and taxis. Yet, by focusing, I was able to fall into a mindful walk even in this place.

Now think about your own life. Where are your "Times Square" places in your life that would present uncommon challenges to practicing mindfulness? Take a moment to prepare for how you could center yourself in the present moment at these times and write down your ideas for future reference.

Gretchen's Outcome

After I worked with Gretchen for three months, her GAD-7 score had fallen to a 3—within the "optimal anxiety" range. She was feeling less irritable and more in control of her mind. In other words, she was back in "the zone." She came to the conclusion that her yoga retreat hadn't increased her worries, but that instead she had just become more aware of them, which had made them feel more prominent.

During this time, she took up swimming, which gave her a chance to be naturally mindful of her breathing. She also persuaded her family to agree to one quiet meal a week, when they stayed mindful of eating and fully enjoyed their food.

Gretchen faced many of the common challenges while establishing her mindfulness practice, but she didn't get discouraged. By our last session, Gretchen had convinced her family to schedule their next annual vacation at a yoga retreat that held a family week, so her loved ones could experience many of the skills we had practiced in our sessions.

. . .

This is our last chapter on skills for your anxiety tool kit. By now, I hope you have

- created a lifestyle that promotes less stress.
- developed your social support network.
- learned to examine—and change—the way you think about your fears.
- become comfortably uncomfortable approaching the fears.
- found ways to reset yourself in the present moment.

But what if these steps aren't enough? Or what if these skills have been somewhat beneficial but, like Gretchen after her retreat, you now feel *more* aware of your worries, stress, and anxiety, and you need more help? Seeking help can be difficult, but the next chapter provides a how-to guide to make it easier.

◆

| 12 |

When You Need More Tools in Your Kit

My patients have had great success in bringing their almost anxiety to manageable levels using the strategies presented in this book—and it's likely that you have already benefited from developing these skills too. But you may be wondering if you need additional tools to help you gain relief from your worries. Here are some questions that people who are almost anxious often ask:

- Is my anxiety severe enough that I should see a mental health care provider?
- How do I make the decision to seek additional help?
- When should I consider taking an antianxiety medication? What are their side effects? How do I decide on the best medication?
- Do any herbal supplements help with anxiety? If so, would they interfere with the medication that I am already taking?

In this chapter, I'll offer some guidelines to help you think through these questions and make educated decisions. Although I'm a psychologist, not a *psychiatrist* (a medical doctor who deals with the mind and can prescribe medications), I can provide a brief overview of the drugs that are available for treating anxiety.

When my patients express a desire to start medications, my recommendation is always for them to visit a psychiatrist who's an expert in anxiety disorders, if at all possible. A onetime consultation might answer your questions and further educate you on your options. If you're interested in seeking more help for your almost anxiety, Lenore's experience might help guide you.

Lenore's Story

Lenore is one of those women who look like she would succeed at almost anything she tries. She's a successful lawyer, a mother of triplets, and (by her husband's own description) a "fantastic" wife. Most of Lenore's childhood had been challenging. She was raised by a single mother in the housing projects of a large city. As a biracial child—Caucasian and African American—Lenore didn't feel that she fit in with either group. This kept her from socializing much. Instead, she focused on academics, which she described as "the only thing I knew I could do by myself." Lenore's schoolwork led her to study at an Ivy League university for her undergrad degree, and then to pursue a law degree.

Lenore described herself as "high-energy, headstrong, and determined." Those were some of the qualities that attracted her husband, Rondo, when they met in college. He had a more easygoing approach to life, pursuing goals at a slow, steady pace. Lenore, on the other hand, spent most of her life "running sprints."

Anxiety had long been a noticeable part of Lenore's character. However, she had found ways to put it to good use. She learned early in life that if she was feeling very anxious, she would become unable to act or make decisions. So she instinctively found ways to keep her anxiety at an optimal level—using methods such as exercise, practicing mindfulness, and staying socially active. She also seemed to have an innate ability both to approach the things that made her anxious and to use anxiety to propel herself to act. Nonetheless, she found herself becoming a bit too anxious at times. Eventually, this led her to my office. She came to see me a year after her triplets were born, telling me, "I can't keep all the balls in the air."

She looked tired, which wasn't surprising. But she was also very angry. She had imagined that this time in her life would be the happiest. After all, now she had everything she had worked so hard her entire life to attain. Rondo was a supportive, involved husband; she had three healthy children; and her career was soaring.

Yet Lenore felt that she couldn't complete most of her tasks at more than a "mediocre" output. Her anxiety had moved past the optimal level, and she was no longer able to contain or capitalize on it. Now her anxiety was driving her life, which left her feeling paralyzed.

A few months earlier, when she first returned to work after maternity leave, she had a mild panic attack. The pounding heart, sweatiness, and dizziness lasted only a few seconds, but Lenore was bothered by them. She discussed the incident with her husband that evening, and she also told her mother and a few co-workers.

In contrast to someone who might go on to develop a full-blown panic disorder, Lenore did not avoid work or significantly change her routine to prevent future panic attacks. She did, however, use subtle ways to avoid panic-like sensations, such as working with her office door open, even if the people talking in the nearby cubicles disrupted her concentration. For Lenore, keeping her door open allowed her to feel that she could escape her office in the event of a panic attack. She would also mentally scan her body on occasion to ensure that she wasn't feeling any odd sensations. But this was not a daily routine.

Lenore hadn't sought any medical attention in response to her panic-like symptoms—which people with full-fledged panic disorders often do—because her husband had continued to reassure her that everything was okay. Yet her old coping strategies, such as exercising, practicing mindfulness, and turning to her friends and family, were no longer balancing out her anxiety. She was feeling stuck.

Lenore asked on her first visit if she could start therapy with me, but she also wanted to know if she should be taking medicine for her anxiety.

Do I Need More Help in Addition to This Book?

Most people have tried-and-true methods that they rely on for managing anxiety, stress, and worries. Usually these work at least some of the time. However, because life stressors wax and wane, it's common for people to have rough patches when their anxiety becomes too much to handle, followed by times when their lives are more balanced and their anxiety and worries subside. Major transitions, for example, can be enough to push people off-center and struggling to cope. Such transitions include both negative and positive events, even happy occasions like having a long-desired baby. At these times, seeking professional guidance can help you find your balance again.

Regardless of where you are on the almost anxious curve, ask yourself the following questions and consider the guidelines given for each when you're deciding whether to consult a mental health care professional.

What Is Your Anxiety Level and How Long Have You Been Here?

At the beginning of the book, I described the GAD-7, which is a simple quiz for diagnosing anxiety and almost anxiety. I used a cutoff score between 5 and 9 to define the almost anxious range. If your score falls within this range and you make a priority of faithfully practicing the skills in this book, odds are good that you won't need to consider additional help at this time.

However, if you've stayed in the almost anxious range for at least six months despite practicing the skills in this book, I would recommend that you seek outside help. A six-month window is consistent with the diagnosis of some anxiety disorders, such as generalized anxiety disorder (GAD), and it's an apt guideline to suggest the need for additional help.

When I first met with her, Lenore scored a 10 on the scale, which is just over the line between almost anxiety and a possible diagnosis for an anxiety disorder. She told me that her past two weeks had been particularly stressful and thought this was why her score might have been so high. When she took the test again a short time later, she scored a 7, which indicated almost anxiety. If we were to plot her scores over the previous few years, we likely would have seen an increase in anxiety right after the birth of her children, followed by a decrease due to her coping skills. Yet in Lenore's case, since her anxiety was significantly interfering with her life, she had done the right thing in seeking help.

What Is Your Social Support Network Suggesting?

Another way to decide whether it's time to seek additional help is to check in with your support system. At times, those around you are better equipped to see when you are struggling than you are. Lenore's husband encouraged her to seek help when he noticed she was unusually anxious. People commonly see me for a consultation not because *they* think they might need help, but because their network is suggesting that they talk to someone. You might suggest that a loved one read this chapter (or the whole book) and then ask what he or she thinks about your situation.

How Often Have You Practiced the Skills in This Book?

I would recommend that you review how much time you've spent using the methods outlined in this book to manage your almost anxiety prior to seeking help. I know that I sometimes forget to practice healthy habits. Recently, for example, I began to be more mindful of my exercise schedule. I started putting stickers on my office calendar on the days that I exercised, without trying to change my routine. Over a month, I was astonished to find that I was averaging only two trips to the gym a week. That was surprising to me since I had felt like I was exercising a *lot*.

It's worth double-checking to see whether you're putting forth your best effort to help yourself with these skills. Use the checklist in exercise 20 for a week, adding a check mark at the end of the day to note the skills you've practiced. (This exercise can be downloaded at www.AlmostAnxious.com.) I would also suggest monitoring your anxiety level by taking the GAD-7 at the beginning of the week and again at the end.

If you notice that you are practicing several of the skills on a daily basis and your anxiety still hasn't decreased at all, then I would recommend seeking additional help. However, if your scores went down, then you might want to consider practicing your new skills for at least another week before seeking professional help.

How to Find a Professional Who Meets Your Needs

If you arrive at the decision that you need additional help, I urge you to ask a few more questions before seeing a mental health care provider.

What Type of Training Does This Professional Have?

If you are going to see a provider for medication, he or she will likely have to be a medical doctor, which means he or she should be licensed in the state where you're seeking care.

Therapists and other types of mental health providers may need different kinds of certification. For example, in some states, providers must have a doctorate degree to call themselves a "licensed clinical psychologist." In other states, regulations are more lenient. I would suggest having an open conversation with your potential provider and asking about his or her training and any certifications or licensing.

Exercise 20.

Anxiety Skills Weekly Monitoring Checklist

DATE / DAY	Eating (Yes/No)	Exercising (Yes/No)	Sleeping (Yes/No)	Broadening Your Social Support (Yes/No)	Examining Your Thinking (Yes/No)	Approaching Your Fears (Yes/No)	Being Mindful (Yes/No)
/ Monday							
/ Tuesday							
/ Wednesday							
/ Thursday							
/ Friday							
/ Saturday							
/ Sunday							

Some of my patients are concerned that they might insult their providers by asking about their training. I personally think that the way providers respond to such questions is a sign of their ability to create a collaborative relationship with patients, which is crucial for a healthy therapeutic alliance. I would strongly urge you to "interview" your provider in a way that is respectful but also provides you with the information you need to decide whether this is a good match. As the conversation goes back and forth, it can suggest how comfortable you would feel discussing your personal issues with this provider.

Has the Provider Treated People with Similar Difficulties?

Most mental health providers, including psychologists and psychiatrists, have a general knowledge of mental health conditions, but they're likely to specialize in some specific disorders and have less expertise in others. If you know that your problems are most likely related to anxiety, then seeking help from someone who specializes in anxiety is a good idea. Here's a similar case in point: I recently had my gallbladder removed by a fantastic surgeon, but after the surgery I had some symptoms that were not resolving with time. I went to see my primary care physician, whom I thoroughly trust and respect. But none of the solutions she suggested worked. Finally, a friend suggested that I go back to the surgeon, since all these problems started after the surgery. Given that I have been working at a major medical center for years, I was surprised that I didn't realize the need to go to the specialist with this problem rather than a doctor who doesn't generally deal with the outcomes of gallbladder surgery. This experience highlighted to me the importance of seeing providers who specialize in the type of case you have, whether physical, mental, or emotional.

Lenore and many of the other people described in this book asked me, "Have you treated others with similar conditions? Based on your experience with other patients, do you think you could help me?" I'd recommend fitting this line of questioning into your interview with a potential provider.

What's the Provider's Proposed Treatment Plan and Diagnosis?

Lenore had never sought treatment before, so she didn't really know what her diagnosis could be. She just knew she was having trouble "managing anxiety and stress."

But you have a little more insight into your situation, having read this book. If you fall within the almost anxious spectrum, you won't meet the diagnosis criteria for any anxiety disorder, yet you still might want to work with a professional. Your provider will need to diagnose you with some type of issue, such as an anxiety disorder, in order to bill an insurance company. In the mental health field, this can be a sore point, since some people might resist having a label. In fact, many individuals with anxiety and related disorders avoid seeking treatment because they are afraid of what others will think.[1]

Yet if you look *outside* the mental health field, most people do want a label! I was relieved when the surgeon explained to me that I had gallstones and not something more serious (or a vague, hard-to-identify source of my symptoms). I didn't want to have surgery, but at least the surgeon had an accurate diagnosis and a proper course of treatment to follow. I am a firm believer that this is the same for anxiety disorders. Although I acknowledge that the diagnosis for emotional difficulties is not as concrete as for gallbladder problems, mental health providers still have many ways to accurately diagnose their patients.

That diagnosis should help guide the course of treatment, which in turn should be driven by research data.

It's fair for you to expect your provider to do the following:

- figure out your "flavor" of anxiety, which is in essence creating a label for it
- tell you about the course of therapy you should anticipate and what skills you will be learning to manage your anxiety
- talk about the evidence supporting this type of therapy for your case

Does This Person Practice Research-Based Treatments?

For years, when people asked what I do for a living, I told them that I was a "behavioral scientist" rather than a psychologist. Although I answered that way to avoid the typical "Are you going to read my mind?" jokes, I also believed that empirical data—or information gathered from studying lots and lots of real people—should drive the way I treat patients. This is particularly important if you are seeking help for almost anxiety, as the efficacy of more generic forms of therapy, such as talk or supportive therapy, have not been studied for any of the anxiety disorders or almost anxiety. That said, several of my patients have benefited from dynamic, less structured types of therapy. Thus, my main concern here is that you find the best help that fits your needs.

There is a caveat, however. It's not uncommon for psychiatrists to prescribe medications that are not FDA-approved for some anxiety and mood disorders; this is called prescribing "off-label." For any type of medication, make sure that your psychiatrist talks to you about these points:

- the type of medication being prescribed
- its usual uses
- why he or she is recommending it for your particular issues, including the benefits you should expect
- when the benefits should become apparent
- short- and long-term risks of side effects
- short- and long-term costs of the treatment
- whether nondrug options might be useful as an alternative or as an add-on treatment with the medication

What Is the Average Length of Treatment for Cases Like Mine?

Unless you're in a research study, it's nearly impossible to predict how long a course of cognitive-behavioral therapy (CBT) will last. However, your provider can follow guidelines based on what research has shown and may be able to give you a rough estimate. I often discuss a time frame with my patients, with the qualification that if they are still working hard in therapy and need more help, I will continue to work with them. At times, things might take a little longer than I originally predicted. As in an exercise program, with CBT—which is the basis for many of the techniques presented in this book—you get back what you put into it. The harder you work, the faster you are likely to get better. I often joke with my patients that my task is to work myself out of a job as fast as possible!

How Will We Measure the Progress of the Therapy?

Taking careful measurements is important when you're trying to improve your health, whether it's your body or mind. That's why the course of your therapy should be monitored. Most people with a fever would feel disconcerted if their doctor didn't take their temperature to ensure that their fever was going down. Yet most of the patients I see are a little surprised by my insistence on monitoring their progress using a data-supported measure, such as the GAD-7. But without careful measurement, our hunches might be incorrect.

So what is the ideal tracking measure for your anxiety? The GAD-7 is a good option. However, not all of my patients welcome the idea of completing a questionnaire every week. In these cases, we come up with other options, like monitoring their mood and anxiety level daily on a scale from 0 (no anxiety) to 10 (the most anxiety). Without some type of measure, it is hard to gauge your progress, so I would encourage you to work with your provider to find a scale that works for both of you.

Do I Need Formal Therapy? Medication? Maybe Both?

These are questions I often answer for patients who are distressed and want to feel better quickly. My answer is simple: one or the other, but if at all possible, *not* both at the same time. In my mind, starting therapy and medication simultaneously for the same problem is like taking two antibiotics for strep throat. You'll most likely get better, but you will never know which one worked. Being a behavioral scientist at heart means I like knowing which solution is behind the beneficial change.

Here's another good reason for taking a one-at-a-time approach: research has shown that although people get better with combined approaches, they do not get twice as much relief, as some might expect. Studies that examined whether people got better faster or more efficiently when following a combined approach compared to either meds or therapy alone found very modest differences between the approaches.

Combining therapy with medication offers little advantage over individual treatments.[2]

I think this principle is much easier to agree with if you fall within the almost spectrum, since you are probably not as distressed as someone with a full-blown anxiety disorder. That said, if your anxiety moves beyond the almost spectrum and into the severe range, you might need to start medication and therapy at the same time. Your provider is the best person to guide you in making this decision.

But if you're choosing one or the other, that leads you to a second question: which option should I use first? On average, if you find the right psychotropic drug, it is likely to work faster for general anxiety than therapy will. As I said, therapy is a lot like going to the gym, and it takes time to build muscles.

Fast-acting medication such as benzodiazepines may provide immediate relief. If that is what you're looking for, then I would suggest starting with medication first, see how far you get with it (making sure to measure your progress), and then if you need more help, you can add therapy.

How Do I Choose the Correct Type of Medication?

Several classes of medication are approved by the FDA for the various anxiety disorders. When it comes to almost anxiety, broadly speaking, there are two main classes: the anxiolytics (such as benzodiazepines) and the antidepressants (such as selective serotonin reuptake inhibitors, or SSRIs). Although they work at different speeds, most of the anxiolytics will provide you with faster relief than the antidepressants, which usually take longer to achieve the optimum therapeutic dosage.

If a patient comes to me who has never taken a quick-acting anxiety-relieving drug such as Xanax, I often discuss the pros and cons of getting a psychiatric consult to consider such medications. On one hand, they are fast-acting drugs, so they will provide relief quickly. On the other hand, I don't want my patients to get the idea that medication is the only way they can manage their problems.

When my patients do opt for the medication route, I refer them to one of my psychiatrist colleagues so they can be educated participants in their own treatment plan. See the "Natural Supplements" sidebar if you or your health care professionals want to explore the option of taking natural supplements and remedies.

Natural Supplements and Remedies for Anxiety Disorders

Although the commonly prescribed antianxiety medications on the market are generally considered safe, some people feel more comfortable trying to manage anxiety with natural remedies first. Although more research is needed on these natural supplements, a 2009 review by Gustavo Kinrys and colleagues, as well as a 2010 review by Shaheen Lakhan and colleagues, highlighted the following remedies for the treatment of anxiety:[3]

St. John's wort may act on dopamine, serotonin, and gamma-aminobutyric acid (GABA), which are brain chemicals that play a central role in mood and anxiety. St. John's wort has been found to be more effective than a placebo at treating mild to moderate depression. In addition, some case studies have shown improvement in people with generalized anxiety disorder after taking this herbal treatment. However, a randomized controlled trial found that St. John's wort was not more effective than a

CONTINUED ON NEXT PAGE

CONTINUED FROM PREVIOUS PAGE

placebo for the treatment of social anxiety disorder. More research on the anxiety-reducing effect of this treatment is needed.[4]

Kava kava, a product of the kava plant, may also have anxiety-reducing effects. Several studies have shown significantly lower anxiety levels in people taking kava compared to a placebo; however, other studies have failed to find this effect. In addition, the FDA has released an advisory that kava kava may cause liver damage.[5]

Passionflower supplements are thought to have an effect on reducing anxiety. Passionflower is also sometimes used to treat sleep disorders.

Valerian root is an herbal remedy that is thought to have sedative effects. It, too, may act on GABA and serotonin. It has been especially effective in studies that combine it with other remedies such as propranolol—a beta-blocker drug—or St. John's wort.

Melatonin, a chemical produced naturally in the brain, is sold as a supplement and is often used as a sleep aid. Although little research has been done on its effect on anxiety, studies looking at anxiety in substance withdrawal suggest it may also have an anxiety-reducing effect.[6]

Inositol is a naturally occurring sugar in our bodies that in some studies reduced the frequency of panic attacks and lowered anxiety scores.[7]

Lysine is an amino acid supplement that may influence neurotransmitters such as GABA, dopamine, serotonin, and norepinephrine. Although more research is needed, lysine supplements have been shown to reduce anxiety scores with no reported side effects.[8]

Some herbal and dietary supplements have side effects and contraindications. In addition, some of these natural remedies should not be taken in combination with other specific substances due to increased risk of adverse reactions or loss of effect. For these reasons, although many of these products are sold over the counter and do not require a prescription, it is highly advisable to check with a health care professional before using these treatments.

Lenore's Outcome

Lenore had thought about meeting with a psychiatrist to discuss whether she should take benzodiazepines, because her anxiety was interfering with her life to a significant degree. However, since she had a strong aversion to taking any medications, she decided to try therapy first.

She started with a process similar to the one I describe in this book, first working on the basics before moving on to cognitive-behavioral therapy approaches. She looked for ways to get Rondo more involved with child rearing so she could dedicate more time to her exercise routine, since she knew that would help reduce her baseline anxiety.

She also developed a more flexible work schedule that could accommodate her new life as a mother of three. She still remained very sleep-deprived, and she had to learn to tell the difference between being physically tired and feeling anxious. One thing that helped Lenore here was to track her sleep, jotting down how many hours she got and how rested she felt in the morning. This tracking helped her realize that (1) not all her bad feelings were related to anxiety and (2) if she was particularly sleep-deprived for a few days, she would need to spend more effort managing her anxiety.

For Lenore's panic-like symptoms, we did some interoceptive exposure so she would become more comfortable with her bodily sensations. For example, I spun her in an office chair and had her hyperventilate into a paper bag until she felt like the resulting sensations weren't scary. (As I mentioned earlier in the book, these are research-supported techniques for the treatment of panic, but they're best conducted with the help of a professional.)

Finally, I worked closely with Lenore to set more realistic self-expectations now that her family had changed. Although she would always be a go-getter, she would need to consider that she had triplets when setting goals for herself to manage her life with less anxiety.

As you can see, Lenore used a wide variety of the skills covered in this book. In the next and final chapter, I'll review all the approaches I've recommended and discuss ways to use your anxiety tool kit for years to come, so you can always capitalize on your anxiety instead of having anxiety run your life.

■ ◆ ■

13

Practicing Skills for a Lifetime

This book has been the culmination of years of work. During my career, I've spent a great deal of time cultivating trust with patients who believed I could serve as a guide in their journey of overcoming their fears and worries. In return, these individuals taught me more about the different approaches that are effective for bringing anxiety and almost anxiety to a healthy level, then focusing it so it becomes fuel for creativity and productivity.

I hope that the skills you've found in these pages have helped you get "unstuck" from your almost anxious wheel. These skills can work for you now, tomorrow, and in years to come. However, it's quite likely that you'll encounter almost anxiety again at some point in your life. Old challenges may resurface. Stressful situations of a new type may arise. Some of the skills you've learned in this book may become rusty from lack of practice, leaving you less protected.

So in this last chapter, I will cover these topics:

- Review the strategies outlined in this book so you can use these tools in combination for the greatest benefit.

- Discuss ways to detect when your anxiety is rising to problem-causing levels.

- Talk about the type of progress you can expect as you use these tools to keep your anxiety levels under control. (Many of my patients think their progress on any issue should be directly related to the effort they put into it. The more time and energy they put into any problem, the better it should get. But life doesn't necessarily work that way. Even if you are dedicated to living a less-anxious life, stressful times can keep your results from being as good as you'd like.)

The story of Isabella, a graduate student I treated years ago, offers a helpful example of how to better connect your skills and put them into practice.

Isabella's Story

The first impression I had of Isabella when I met her on a hot summer day was that she was warm, polite, and a pleasure to be around.

In her mid-thirties, Isabella was pursuing her doctoral degree in mathematics at a local college. Her parents lived in one of Boston's suburbs, and she was very involved with them. Whenever life got tough, especially academically, Isabella would reach out to her family, particularly her father, a high school teacher who had once dreamed of pursuing a doctorate in mathematics himself.

Although she was friendly, Isabella avoided eye contact

during our first session, as though she felt ashamed to be sitting in my office. This was her first encounter with the mental health profession, and she was unsure whether she actually needed help. I'd agreed to consult with her and to assess whether she indeed had an issue that could benefit from therapy and, if so, whether my skills as a cognitive-behavioral therapist were a good match for her.

Isabella explained that she had always been shy, but she had managed to maintain a small group of friends throughout her life. In addition to feeling close to her family and friends, her academic advisor and classmates were sources of support. Being the only woman in her doctoral class felt slightly isolating to her, but she hadn't let it deter her from her goals.

Still, she had some problems that she wanted to address. Her anxiety was rising to a level that she deemed "unacceptable" in several areas of her life. First, Isabella was starting to feel like a prisoner of her performance anxiety. She had always disliked public speaking, but as she advanced in her career, she was receiving more invitations to speak in public (mathematicians do more than just figure out equations on their own!). She would accept the invitations, then prepare, overprepare, and then prepare some more, memorizing each line that she would say during a talk. This process was exhausting to her. She started to notice that speaking led to a lot of ramped-up energy and sleepless nights, followed by a crash after a presentation, with a sense that she had spent her "life force" on the talk. Isabella didn't want to stop presenting her work at academic meetings, but she was starting to feel as though she needed to avoid them, given the emotional cost that came with each presentation.

The second reason Isabella sought me out was because she

was having trouble dating. Given her age, she felt she was running out of time for having a family of her own. But it wasn't clear to her what she could do about it. Like many graduate students, she spent much of her time on campus working on her research. This left little time in her schedule for dating and other social events. Though most of the graduate students and professors surrounding her were men, she didn't want to date any of them. "It would be too hard to mix work and my romantic life. You know, what if things didn't work out?" she explained.

Her primary fear with public speaking was that people would think she was stupid (which is much like the symptoms of the social subtype of almost anxiety). However, her dating fears were not about being judged negatively. Rather, she worried that she wouldn't be able to balance a future family with academic life. "I want a husband and a family, but I also want to have a career, and I'm afraid that I will have to sacrifice one for the other," she said. I sensed that, even with her busy schedule, Isabella could have found some time for dating. It seemed that her fear that the two elements in her life were incompatible was what had kept her from putting herself into the dating world. In essence, I suspected that she was avoiding.

Since she was focusing primarily on research during the summer and not taking classes, she had some extra time to tend to her personal life. So we decided to work together on helping her find ways to become more comfortable with speaking situations and to start dating again. Following are the steps that Isabella and I worked through. As you address issues that affect your own almost anxiety, I suggest you use these steps as well.

Step 1: Looking at Her Almost Anxious Wheel

Isabella and I began by developing a full understanding of how her almost anxiety–related thoughts, feelings, and actions traveled around in a circle. She took the quizzes for worry, social, and physical feelings that are described in chapter 4, and we used the information to create her almost anxious hamster wheel. The results of the quizzes suggested that we needed to focus on her speaking fears, since this problem was creating the most immediate distress in her life.

We looked at Isabella's most recent presentation to determine where she would enter the almost anxious wheel and what factors got her stuck. Fortunately, she had given a talk only a few weeks prior to this session, so the memories were still fresh in her mind. Here's how our conversation on this issue transpired.

Isabella: It was a presentation at our national conference. Many of the world's most prominent mathematicians were there. I was a speaker in a symposium with my academic advisor. Until a few days before the talk, he was going to be giving the presentation, so I was not worried about it. However, his wife just had their third child, and he requested that I take his place.

Dr. M.: What happened when he asked you to give the talk? What were you thinking about?

Isabella: Thinking? There was no thinking involved! I just got really anxious, my mouth went dry, my heart started to pound, I started to shake, and I felt scared.

Dr. M.: So it sounds like the first thing that happened is that your body had a physical response to the idea of the presentation: you had a dry mouth, increased heart rate, and shakiness. It also sounds like you had a lot of feeling attached to your response, primarily things like fear and anxiety.

Isabella: You're right! I was really scared and just wanted to tell him that I couldn't do it.

Dr. M.: That makes a lot of sense. You felt a looming sense of danger, and you wanted to do anything to try to stop those uncomfortable sensations and feelings. The easiest way to do that would be to avoid it completely. In this case, you wanted to tell your advisor that you could not do it. Did you do that, Isabella?

Isabella: No. *(Deep sigh.)* I knew that he had been looking forward to presenting our results and that this meant a lot to him. I also really like his wife and didn't want her to feel bad that he couldn't be there for her and their baby. I am not sure what I actually said in that moment. I was having a hard time focusing, but I agreed to do it.

Dr. M.: So, despite all your fears and your body reacting to the idea, you still decided to say yes? That must have been difficult! What happened next?

Isabella: The next few days leading up to the conference were a blur. I must have practiced the talk a million times. I know I called my family a lot to ask them if they thought I could do it. I also kept analyzing our numbers, just in case someone were to ask a question that I couldn't answer. The interesting thing was, the more I practiced, the worse my anxiety got and the more I called my parents. I think they were annoyed with me, but they are too polite to show it. I sure know that my lab mate who was attending the conference with me got aggravated.

Dr. M.: Before we put this on your almost anxious hamster wheel, I would like to know if any thoughts kept coming up and scaring you when you thought about the presentation? What were you *saying to yourself* as the day approached?

Isabella: I guess I was thinking that I would embarrass myself or sound stupid or, even worse, I might not be able to give the presentation, which would mean that I would let everyone down. What if that caused me to get kicked out of the program? That would be a disaster! *(Starts to cry.)*

Dr. M.: Isabella, it sounds like you had a lot of catastrophic thoughts that were predicting the worst, and I can imagine that you even had a visual picture of that happening. I can see how upsetting that would have been for you. Let's take a moment and put this together in the almost anxious wheel and learn about how you are getting stuck when it comes to your public-speaking fears.

Figure 23.

Isabella's Almost Anxious Wheel

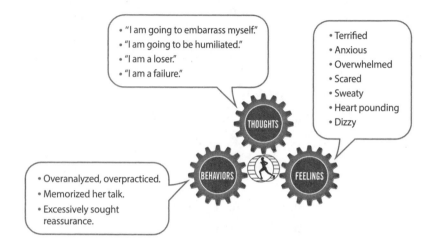

Isabella was entering the almost anxious wheel through her physical sensations and emotions (see figure 23). That was what set the wheel in motion. Once her advisor asked her to shoulder the presentation, she had a "false alarm" physical response, which came with lots of emotions.

Step 2: Cleaning Up Her Lifestyle

I also wanted to make sure that Isabella's "engine" was firing on all cylinders, so we spent a few weeks regulating her sleep and exercise routines. Neither of these issues alone might have raised Isabella's anxiety to an upsetting level, but together they certainly could have been contributing to it. Isabella already ate a healthy diet, so we didn't have to change anything there.

Her sleep schedule was completely unregulated. At first, Isabella didn't want to try any of the sleep-improvement strategies I suggested; sleep hygiene was not a priority for her. She felt like she did her best work at night, she said. But with time, she started to see how her erratic sleep schedule affected her level of anxiety. After a few weeks, she shifted to a sleep pattern that was ideal for her. Though she was still a "night owl," she now avoided scheduling activities early in the morning so she could get enough sleep, which for her amounted to seven hours. (When it comes to sleep, get enough for *your* needs rather than following someone else's pattern.)

Also, since beginning graduate school, she had stopped taking the daily swims that she had been doing for most of her life. Now Isabella began setting aside time for swimming, which she was able to do at lunchtime three days a week. Although this exercise didn't reduce her almost anxiety related to public speaking, it did bring down her overall baseline levels, which helped us when it came time to approach some of her feared situations.

Step 3: Recognizing That Avoidance—Not the Anxiety— Is the Enemy!

Sorting through her subtle avoidance, reassurance, and social support, I found that although Isabella's innate desire was to avoid, that was nearly impossible if she wanted to continue with her academic career. So Isabella had to white-knuckle through the challenge. Each time she has given a talk, she has felt a great deal of anticipatory anxiety, mostly fueled by catastrophic thinking. She has typically engaged in fortune telling by predicting that the worst would happen and that she wouldn't be able to handle it.

Even as she racked up these presentations, Isabella's experience didn't change, which was puzzling to her. "Why is it that I don't get used to it?" she asked. I could see why: she was engaging in a bunch of subtle avoidance strategies that were keeping her stuck and preventing her from having the experiences that could correct her reaction.

Isabella's overt and subtle avoidance strategies included these:

- overpreparing for the talk, including trying to memorize every word she would say during the presentation
- excessively asking for reassurance before the talk
- bringing a trusted colleague to the talk to make herself feel better
- avoiding eye contact with audience members during the talk
- avoiding things that would make her jittery, like coffee

These strategies probably helped Isabella in the short term, since she didn't think she would ever be able to give a presentation without them. Yet they had devastating long-term consequences. They maintained her distorted belief that she would embarrass herself or sound stupid during her presentations. Plus, they kept her from trusting that she could succeed on her own without these routines.

One of our goals in therapy was to identify all of Isabella's avoidance strategies so that we could work on them through exposure therapy. Isabella's social support—specifically her parents—was a central part of her avoidance. Isabella was fortunate that she was very close to her family, and they provided a great deal of support. However, in their attempts to love and help her, her parents were also fostering her anxiety by providing reassurance.

By this time, Isabella was already convinced that avoidance was the issue that was impairing her life. So she and I had a long discussion about how excessive reassurance seeking was a form of avoidance. She eventually approached her parents and created a "contract" with them about the amount of reassurance it was reasonable for them to provide when she called feeling distressed about an upcoming talk.

Isabella also discussed the role of reassurance with her academic advisor and some of her graduate school friends. All of them were understanding (yet a bit puzzled), and they agreed to refrain from giving her excessive reassurance before, during, or after her academic presentations.

Step 4: Balancing Her Thinking

When public speaking obligations arose, distorted thoughts surfaced in Isabella's mind:

- I will do something embarrassing.
- I will sound stupid.
- I won't be able to finish the presentation, because I am too anxious.
- I will get kicked out of my academic program.

Isabella was catastrophizing, fortune telling, and labeling herself in a negative manner. We used exercise 17, "Challenging Your Anxiety-Fueled Thinking," from chapter 9 to help her challenge her thinking and shift to more balanced thoughts. For example, after reviewing the evidence, which included always being able to give presentations when needed and often receiving praise for them afterward, she was able to arrive at a more balanced conclusion: "Even though I feel anxious, I have no evidence to suggest that my fears will come true. In fact, I only have evidence *against* it."

Isabella was also having trouble finding the time and motivation for dating. One way we dealt with this concern was by making use of Isabella's social support system. She identified three girlfriends who were not part of her academic program and asked them to be her "dating advisors." They were tasked with encouraging her to be more social and to date more. Isabella also realized that spending every weekend visiting her parents was a way that she avoided dating. So she started reserving "dating weekends," when her primary focus would be to spend time going out with men.

Step 5: Approaching Her Lions

Exposing yourself to the things that cause you fear (that is, approaching your "lions" in a comfortably uncomfortable way) is often necessary when you want your anxiety to work for you. Isabella was puzzled by the thought of exposure therapy. After all, she had been "exposed" to giving presentations before. How could speaking more help her get better?

So Isabella and I went through the steps of creating an anxiety hierarchy, as discussed in chapter 10, and we discussed why white-knuckling through talks isn't actually exposure therapy. Her hierarchy started with giving presentations at less-prominent meetings. Also, we took away all of Isabella's safety behaviors, including her reassurance seeking, bringing friends to talks, and overpreparing. For exposure to work, it's usually best if done gradually so it's more tolerable. Accordingly, Isabella climbed up her hierarchy slowly. By the end of our work together, she was about to give a presentation at an important international gathering without seeking reassurance from anyone and after practicing it just once. She later reported that it went really well.

Isabella used the same framework to continue her improvement in dating. She joined an online dating site, and for a while she approached it with the spirit of "practicing"—not because she was fearful of men, but because she hadn't dated recently and wanted to get more comfortable with it. She relied heavily on her dating support system to approach this. As with her time in the swimming pool, she had to learn to create space for dating in her busy schedule.

Step 6: Making Time for Mindfulness

Isabella wasn't interested in developing a meditation practice. However, after much discussion, she suggested that swimming was a way for her to remain mindful. She noticed that she was very attentive to her breathing while she was swimming, which in turn left her feeling better and more centered after she got out of the pool. That made sense to me, and it taught me an important lesson about meditation.

It's best to find a creative way to integrate meditation into your life, rather than forcing it in awkwardly or making yourself do something you don't really enjoy. This will increase the meditation's effectiveness. It will also help you maintain the practice for longer. The same goes for all the advice in this book: find ways to make these strategies work in your own life. I've provided cases throughout the book in which these methods were effective for other people, but it's important to adapt them to your own particular needs.

Stressful and challenging situations aren't going to stop

cropping up. They're going to be a regular presence in your life, my life, and everyone else's life. So make sure you practice all of the strategies in your almost anxiety tool kit regularly. Doing so will help keep your anxiety at a healthy level from day to day, and these tools will also help you handle bigger problems that arise from time to time.

Almost Anxiety Strategies

Step 1: Look at your almost anxious wheel.

Step 2: Clean up your lifestyle.

Step 3: Recognize that avoidance—not the anxiety— is the enemy.

Step 4: Balance your thinking.

Step 5: Approach your lions.

Step 6: Make time for mindfulness.

Taming Your Almost Anxiety for Life

I'd like to leave you with a few additional thoughts on understanding how these skills work and what happens when they seem to stop working.

Keep Appropriate Expectations

Isabella was a scientist, and her experience taught her that the more attention she paid to an experiment, the more precise it was (and the more efficient she would be at future experiments). As such, she had the expectation that if she practiced the skills we were discussing "perfectly," she would manage her almost anxiety more quickly. Additionally, Isabella predicted that she would only keep "getting better," so she found herself feeling very discouraged when she hit a bump in her progress.

This is common for everyone I treat, and I've witnessed it in my own life. These expectations are unrealistic, and they set you up for failure. When it comes to practicing a new skill— any new skill, including cognitive and behavioral principles— you'll need to fine-tune your approach as you move along. While practice is necessary for success, don't expect progress to be even. You may find you are taking the proverbial "two steps forward and one step back." Nor should you anticipate that your level of anxiety will continue to get closer to the ideal year after year. This brings me to another point.

Dealing with Lapses

Progress in managing anxiety doesn't move along a straight line heading upward. Expect some backsliding along the way. Who hasn't been really good about following their diet for a long period, only to find themselves in trouble during the holidays?

It's less important that you have a slip, which psychologists call a "lapse," than what you do about it. When a lapse occurs, it's crucial to keep it from turning into a full relapse—that is, to prevent your anxiety symptoms from reverting to their most severe level. That's because relapses take longer to fix, since you often have to start from the ground up again. One of my patients, Arun, is a case in point.

Arun's Story

Arun came in for a booster session because he was afraid he was starting to relapse. I had treated Arun for panic-related anxiety, as well as some health anxiety concerns, both of which were triggered when he felt physically ill, such as when he had a cold.

A few weeks before he came back in, Arun had picked up a cold virus while visiting his wife's family for the holidays. This led him to wonder: "What if something else is seriously wrong with me?" He then avoided anything that might trigger panic-like sensations, such as skiing during the trip.

During this lapse, Arun worked hard on the skills we had practiced during treatment, but he was still feeling edgy a few weeks after he returned from the holidays. He was afraid that he would end up in a full relapse.

After discussing how his situation had progressed, we brainstormed ways that Arun could have tried to prevent getting stuck on the almost anxious wheel, such as making time to write down his thoughts and challenge them while he was experiencing a temporarily heightened level of anxiety. Additionally, we touched on the relationship between anxiety and physical illnesses, and we discussed whether some of the symptoms he was attributing to relapse weren't better accounted for by the cold or perhaps by a combination of preexisting vulnerability to panic in addition to having the cold. By the time we finished our session, Arun was confident that he had the skills he needed to keep practicing and that his lapse was only a blip in his therapy progress.

Here are some ways to catch lapses early:

- Continue to monitor your progress, as discussed in the previous chapter, and take action as soon as you see any signs of heightened anxiety or, even more important, signs of avoidance creeping back in.
- When you notice that you are moving toward a lapse, review this book and take a fresh look at the strategies throughout.

Figure 24.
Isabella's Skills Checklist

	THOUGHTS	FEELINGS/ PHYSICAL SENSATIONS	BEHAVIOR/AVOIDANCE
Chapter 6: Anxiety or Avoidance: Focus on the True Enemy			✓
Chapter 7: Let's Get Physical!		✓	
Chapter 8: Tapping Into the Power of Your Social Network		✓	
Chapter 9: Challenge Your Anxiety-Fueled Way of Thinking	✓		
Chapter 10: It's Time to Feel Comfortably Uncomfortable		✓	✓
Chapter 11: Be Here Now	✓		

- If those steps aren't enough, consider seeking additional help, as outlined in chapter 12.

Isabella's Outcome—and *Yours*

Isabella is now happily married to a pediatrician and about to give birth to their first child. Each of the skills highlighted in figure 24 ensured Isabella's success in therapy.

As we come to the end of this book, I hope it represents a new beginning for you—a beginning of a life in which you have a reasonable amount of anxiety that propels you forward rather than holds you back.

Throughout this book, I shared composite stories of the many patients who were kind enough to share their own journeys with me and to trust me to guide them along new routes. Science backs up all the suggestions that I provided to them, and to you. I hope you'll be able to adjust these strategies so they fit seamlessly into your life.

In graduate school, many clinical psychologists read an article by psychology professor Phil Kendall that encourages beginner therapists to "breathe life into the manual."[1] That means we need to apply flexibility to the treatment manuals that we follow so they can be relevant to the patients we're trying to help. This book is my attempt to breathe life into the skills that have helped millions of individuals through my own practice and through the practice of my colleagues around the world. After discussing them in this conversation with you, I hope these skills help you catch your almost anxiety early on and perhaps avoid the slippery slope that leads to full-fledged anxiety disorders.

If you take just one lesson from this book, I hope it is the knowledge that you can begin living your life more in the present moment, approaching—not avoiding—your fears in a *comfortably uncomfortable* way!

· ◆ ·

appendix

DSM-5 Diagnoses

Criteria are reprinted from the American Psychiatric Association's *Diagnostic and Statistical Manual of Mental Disorders, 5th edition* (Washington, DC: APA, 2013). Reprint permission pending.

Generalized Anxiety Disorder

A. Excessive anxiety and worry (apprehensive expectation), occurring more days than not for at least 6 months, about a number of events or activities (such as work or school performance).

B. The individual finds it difficult to control the worry.

C. The anxiety and worry are associated with three (or more) of the following six symptoms (with at least some symptoms having been present for more days than not for the past 6 months). (**Note:** Only one item is required in children.)

 1. Restlessness or feeling keyed up or on edge.

 2. Being easily fatigued.

 3. Difficulty concentrating or mind going blank.

4. Irritability.

5. Muscle tension.

6. Sleep disturbance (difficulty falling or staying asleep, or restless, unsatisfying sleep).

D. The anxiety, worry, or physical symptoms cause clinically significant distress or impairment in social, occupational, or other important areas of functioning.

E. The disturbance is not attributable to the physiological effects of a substance (e.g., a drug of abuse, a medication) or another medical condition (e.g., hyperthyroidism).

F. The disturbance is not better explained by another mental disorder (e.g., anxiety or worry about having panic attacks in panic disorder, negative evaluation in social anxiety disorder, contamination or other obsessions in obsessive-compulsive disorder, separation from attachment figures in separation anxiety disorder, reminders of traumatic events in posttraumatic stress disorder, gaining weight in anorexia nervosa, physical complaints in somatic symptom disorder, perceived appearance flaws in body dysmorphic disorder, having a serious illness in illness anxiety disorder, or the content of delusional beliefs in schizophrenia or delusional disorder).

Panic Disorder Criteria

A. Recurrent unexpected panic attacks. A panic attack is an abrupt surge of intense fear or intense discomfort that reaches a peak within minutes, and during which time four (or more) of the following symptoms occur:

Note: The abrupt surge can occur from a calm state or an anxious state.

1. Palpitations, pounding heart, or accelerated heart rate.
2. Sweating.
3. Trembling or shaking.
4. Sensations of shortness of breath or smothering.
5. Feelings of choking.
6. Chest pain or discomfort.
7. Nausea or abdominal distress.
8. Feeling dizzy, unsteady, lightheaded, or faint.
9. Chills or heat sensations.
10. Paresthesias (numbness or tingling sensations).
11. Derealization (feelings of unreality) or depersonalization (being detached from oneself).
12. Fear of losing control or "going crazy."
13. Fear of dying.

Note: Culture-specific symptoms (e.g., tinnitus, neck soreness, headache, uncontrollable screaming or crying) may be seen. Such symptoms should not count as one of the four required symptoms.

B. At least one of the attacks has been followed by 1 month (or more) of one or both of the following:

1. Persistent concern or worry about additional panic attacks or their consequences (e.g., losing control, having a heart attack, "going crazy").
2. A significant maladaptive change in behavior related to the attacks (e.g., behaviors designed to avoid having

panic attacks, such as avoidance of exercise or unfamiliar situations).

C. The disturbance is not attributable to the physiological effects of a substance (e.g., a drug of abuse, a medication) or another medical condition (e.g., hyperthyroidism, cardiopulmonary disorders).

D. The disturbance is not better explained by another mental disorder (e.g., the panic attacks do not occur only in response to feared social situations, as in social anxiety disorder; in response to circumscribed phobic objects or situations, as in specific phobia; in response to obsessions, as in obsessive-compulsive disorder; in response to reminders of traumatic events, as in posttraumatic stress disorder; or in response to separation from attachment figures, as in separation anxiety disorder).

Specific Phobia Criteria

A. Marked fear or anxiety about a specific object or situation (e.g., flying, heights, animals, receiving an injection, seeing blood). (**Note:** In children, the fear or anxiety may be expressed by crying, tantrums, freezing, or clinging.)

B. The phobic object or situation almost always provokes immediate fear or anxiety.

C. The phobic object or situation is actively avoided or endured with intense fear or anxiety.

D. The fear or anxiety is out of proportion to the actual danger posed by the specific object or situation and to the sociocultural context.

E. The fear, anxiety, or avoidance is persistent, typically lasting for 6 months or more.

F. The fear, anxiety, or avoidance causes clinically significant distress or impairment in social, occupational, or other important areas of functioning.

G. The disturbance is not better explained by the symptoms of another mental disorder, including fear, anxiety, and avoidance of situations associated with panic-like symptoms or other incapacitating symptoms (as in agoraphobia); objects or situations related to obsessions (as in obsessive-compulsive disorder); reminders of traumatic events (as in posttraumatic stress disorder); separation from home or attachment figures (as in separation anxiety disorder); or social situations (as in social anxiety disorder).

Agoraphobia Criteria

A. Marked fear or anxiety about two (or more) of the following five situations:

1. Using public transportation (e.g., automobiles, buses, trains, ships, planes).

2. Being in open spaces (e.g., parking lots, market places, or bridges).

3. Being in enclosed places (e.g., shops, theaters, or cinemas).

4. Standing in line or being in a crowd.

5. Being outside of the home alone.

B. The individual fears or avoids these situations because of thoughts that escape might be difficult or help might not be available in the event of developing panic-like symptoms or other incapacitating symptoms (e.g., fear of falling in the elderly; fear of incontinence).

C. The agoraphobic situations almost always provoke fear or anxiety.

D. The agoraphobic situations are actively avoided, require the presence of a companion, or are endured with marked fear or anxiety.

E. The fear or anxiety is out of proportion to the actual danger posed by the agoraphobic situations and to the sociocultural context.

F. The fear, anxiety, or avoidance is persistent, typically lasting for 6 months or more.

G. The fear, anxiety, or avoidance causes clinically significant distress or impairment in social, occupational, or other important areas of functioning.

H. If another medical condition (e.g., inflammatory bowel disease, Parkinson's disease) is present, the fear, anxiety, or avoidance is clearly excessive.

I. The fear, anxiety, or avoidance is not better explained by the symptoms of another mental disorder—for example, the symptoms are not confined to specific phobia, situational type; do not involve only social situations (as in social anxiety disorder); and are not related exclusively to obsessions (as in obsessive-compulsive disorder), perceived defects or flaws in physical appearance (as in body dysmorphic disorder), reminders or traumatic events (as in posttraumatic stress disorder), or fear of separation (as in separation anxiety disorder).

Note: Agoraphobia is diagnosed irrespective of the presence of panic disorder. If an individual's presentation meets criteria for panic disorder and agoraphobia, both diagnoses should be assigned.

Social Anxiety Disorder Criteria

A. Marked fear or anxiety about one or more social situations in which the individual is exposed to possible scrutiny by others. Examples include social interactions (e.g., having a conversation, meeting unfamiliar people), being observed (e.g., eating or drinking), and performing in front of others (e.g., giving a speech).

   Note: In children, the anxiety must occur in peer settings and not just during interactions with adults.

B. The individual fears that he or she will act in a way or show anxiety symptoms that will be negatively evaluated (i.e., will be humiliating or embarrassing; will lead to rejection or offend others).

C. The social situations almost always provoke fear or anxiety. (**Note:** In children, the fear or anxiety may be expressed by crying, tantrums, freezing, clinging, shrinking, or failing to speak in social situations.)

D. The social situations are avoided or endured with intense fear or anxiety.

E. The fear or anxiety is out of proportion to the actual threat posed by the social situation and to the socio-cultural context.

F. The fear, anxiety, or avoidance is persistent, typically lasting for 6 months or more.

G. The fear, anxiety, or avoidance causes clinically significant distress or impairment in social, occupational, or other important areas of functioning.

H. The fear, anxiety, or avoidance is not attributable to the physiological effects of a substance (e.g., a drug of abuse, a medication) or another medical condition.

I. The fear, anxiety, or avoidance is not better explained by the symptoms of another mental disorder, such as panic disorder, body dysmorphic disorder, or autism spectrum disorder.

J. If another medical condition (e.g., Parkinson's disease, obesity, disfigurement from burns or injury) is present, the fear, anxiety, or avoidance is clearly unrelated or is excessive. *Specify* as **"performance only"** if the fear is restricted to speaking or performing in public.

notes

Introduction: Even a *Little* Too Much Anxiety Is a Problem Worth Solving

1. E. D. Eaker, L. M. Sullivan, M. Kelly-Hayes, R. B. D'Agostino Sr., and E. J. Benjamin, "Tension and Anxiety and the Prediction of the 10-Year Incidence of Coronary Heart Disease, Atrial Fibrillation, and Total Mortality: The Framingham Offspring Study," *Psychosomatic Medicine* 67, no. 5 (2005): 692–96.

Chapter 1: What Is "Almost Anxious"?

1. National Park Service, "Yosemite," 2012, www.nps.gov/yose/index.htm.

2. R. C. Kessler, W. T. Chiu, R. Jin, A. M. Ruscio, K. Shear, and E. E. Walters, "The Epidemiology of Panic Attacks, Panic Disorder, and Agoraphobia in the National Comorbidity Survey Replication," *Archives of General Psychiatry* 63, no. 4 (2006): 415–24.

3. R. M. Yerkes and J. D. Dodson, "The Relation of Strength of Stimulus to Rapidity of Habit-Formation," *Journal of Comparative Neurology and Psychology* 15, no. 5 (1908): 459–82.

4. J. Karsten, W. A. Nolen, B. W. J. H. Penninx, and C. A. Hartman, "Subthreshold Anxiety Better Defined by Symptom Self-Report Than by Diagnostic Interview," *Journal of Affective Disorders* 129, no. 1 (2011): 236–43.

5. R. L. Spitzer, K. Kroenke, J. B. W. Williams, and B. Löwe, "A Brief Measure for Assessing Generalized Anxiety Disorder: The GAD-7," *Archives of Internal Medicine* 166, no. 10 (2006): 1092–97.

6. M. A. Ruiz, E. Zamorano, J. García-Campayo, A. Pardo, O. Freire, and J. Rejas, "Validity of the GAD-7 Scale as an Outcome Measure of Disability in Patients with Generalized Anxiety Disorders in Primary Care," *Journal of Affective Disorders* 128, no. 3 (2011): 277–86.

7. Spitzer et al., "A Brief Measure for Assessing Generalized Anxiety Disorder," 1092–127.

8. B. Löwe, O. Decker, S. Müller, E. Brähler, D. Schellberg, W. Herzog, and P. Y. Herzberg, "Validation and Standardization of the Generalized Anxiety Disorder Screener (GAD-7) in the General Population," *Medical Care* 46, no. 3 (2008): 266–74.

9. A. Bystritsky, L. Kerwin, N. Niv, J. L. Natoli, N. Abrahami, R. Klap, K. Wells, and A. S. Young, "Clinical and Subthreshold Panic Disorder," *Depression and Anxiety* 27, no. 4 (2010): 381–89.

10. L. Fehm, K. Beesdo, F. Jacobi, and A. Fiedler, "Social Anxiety Disorder Above and Below the Diagnostic Threshold: Prevalence, Comorbidity and Impairment in the General Population," *Social Psychiatry and Psychiatric Epidemiology* 43, no. 4 (2008): 257–65; A. S. Filho, L. A. Hetem, M. C. Ferrari, C. Trzesniak, R. Martín-Santos, T. Borduqui, F. de Lima Osório, S. R. Loureiro, G. Filho Busatto, A. W. Zuardi, and J. A. Crippa, "Social Anxiety Disorder: What Are We Losing with the Current Diagnostic Criteria?" *Acta Psychiatrica Scandinavica* 121, no. 3 (2010): 216–26.

11. A. Gangemi, F. Mancini, and M. van den Hout, "Behavior as Information: 'If I Avoid, Then There Must Be a Danger,'" *Journal of Behavior Therapy and Experimental Psychiatry* 43, no. 4 (2012): 1032–38.

12. M. W. Otto, D. F. Tolin, K. R. Nations, A. C. Utschig, B. O. Rothbaum, S. G. Hofmann, and J. A. Smits, "Five Sessions and Counting: Considering Ultra-Brief Treatment for Panic Disorder," *Depression and Anxiety* 29, no. 6 (2012): 465–70.

Chapter 2: The Many "Flavors" of Anxiety

1. American Psychiatric Association, "DSM-5: The Future of Psychiatric Diagnosis," 2012, www.dsm5.org/Pages/Default.aspx.

2. D. J. Stein, N. A. Fineberg, O. J. Bienvenu, D. Denys, C. Lochner, G. Nestadt, J. F. Leckman, S. L. Rauch, and K. A. Phillips, "Should OCD Be Classified as an Anxiety Disorder in DSM-V?" *Depression and Anxiety* 27, no. 6 (2010): 495–506.

3. L. Marques, D. J. Robinaugh, N. J. LeBlanc, and D. Hinton, "Cross-Cultural Variations in the Prevalence and Presentation of Anxiety Disorders," *Expert Review of Neurotherapeutics* 11, no. 2 (2011): 313–22.

4. R. C. Kessler, M. Angermeyer, J. C. Anthony, R. Graaf, K. Demyttenaere, I. Gasquet, G. Girolamo, S. Gluzman, O. Gureje, J. M. Haro, N. Kawakami, A. Karam, D. Levinson, M. E. Medina Mora, M. A. Oakley Browne, J. Posada-Villa, D. J. Stein, C. H. Adley Tsang, S. Aguilar-Gaxiola, J. Alonso, S. Lee, S. Heeringa, B. E. Pennell, P. Berglund, M. J. Gruber,

M. Petukhova, S. Chatterji, and T. B. Ustün, "Lifetime Prevalence and Age-of-Onset Distributions of Mental Disorders in the World Health Organization's World Mental Health Survey Initiative," *World Psychiatry* 6, no. 3 (2007): 168–76.

5. T. H. Ollendick, B. Yang, N. J. King, Q. Dong, and A. Akande, "Fears in American, Australian, Chinese, and Nigerian Children and Adolescents: A Cross-Cultural Study," *Journal of Child Psychology and Psychiatry* 37, no. 2 (1996): 213–20.

6. M. Sierra-Siegert and A. S. David, "Depersonalization and Individualism: The Effect of Culture on Symptom Profiles in Panic Disorder," *Journal of Nervous and Mental Disease* 195, no. 12 (2007): 989–95.

7. Marques et al., "Cross-Cultural Variations," 313–22.

8. R. C. Kessler, M. Petukhova, N. A. Sampson, A. M. Zaslavsky, and H. U. Wittchen, "Twelve-Month and Lifetime Prevalence and Lifetime Morbid Risk of Anxiety and Mood Disorders in the United States," *International Journal of Methods in Psychiatric Research* 21, no. 3 (2012): 169–84.

9. Ibid.

10. Ibid.

11. Ibid.

12. I. M. Aderka, S. G. Hofmann, A. Nickerson, H. Hermesh, E. Gilboa-Schechtman, and S. Marom, "Functional Impairment in Social Anxiety Disorder," *Journal of Anxiety Disorders* 26, no. 3 (2012): 393–400; E. Moitra, C. Beard, R. B. Weisberg, and M. B. Keller, "Occupational Impairment and Social Anxiety Disorder in a Sample of Primary Care Patients," *Journal of Affective Disorders* 130, no. 1–2 (2011): 209–12.

13. Kessler et al., "Twelve-Month and Lifetime Prevalence," 169–84.

14. American Psychiatric Association, "DSM-5: The Future of Psychiatric Diagnosis," 2012, www.dsm5.org/Pages/Default.aspx.

15. S. G. Hofmann and J. A. J. Smits, "Cognitive-Behavioral Therapy for Adult Anxiety Disorders: A Meta-Analysis of Randomized Placebo-Controlled Trials," *Journal of Clinical Psychiatry* 69, no. 4 (2008): 621–32.

Chapter 3: Am I Almost Anxious ... *and* Something Else?

1. E. A. Mayer, "Clinical Practice. Irritable Bowel Syndrome," *New England Journal of Medicine* 358, no. 16 (2008): 1692–99.

2. D. F. Gros, M. M. Antony, R. E. McCabe, and R. P. Swinson, "Frequency and Severity of the Symptoms of Irritable Bowel Syndrome across the

Anxiety Disorders and Depression," *Journal of Anxiety Disorders* 23, no. 2 (2009): 290–96.

3. R. B. Lydiard, "Psychopharmacology in the Treatment of Irritable Bowel Syndrome," *Primary Psychiatry* 14, no. 4 (2007): 41–42, 45–50.

4. G. J. G. Asmundson, D. K. Larsen, and M. B. Stein, "Panic Disorder and Vestibular Disturbance: An Overview of Empirical Findings and Clinical Implications," *Journal of Psychosomatic Research* 44, no. 1 (1998): 107–20; N. M. Simon, D. Blacker, N. B. Korbly, S. G. Sharma, J. J. Worthington, M. W. Otto, and M. H. Pollack, "Hypothyroidism and Hyperthyroidism in Anxiety Disorders Revisited: New Data and Literature Review," *Journal of Affective Disorders* 69, no. 1–3 (2002): 209–17.

5. J. R. Britton, "Maternal Anxiety: Course and Antecedents during the Early Postpartum Period," *Depression and Anxiety* 25, no. 9 (2008): 793–800.

6. Asmundson, Larsen, and Stein, "Panic Disorder and Vestibular Disturbance," 107–20.

7. A. B. Raj and D. V. Sheehan, "Mitral Valve Prolapse and Panic Disorder," *Bulletin of the Menninger Clinic* 54, no. 2 (1990): 199–208; M. Craske and D. H. Barlow, "Panic Disorder and Agoraphobia," in *Clinical Handbook of Psychological Disorders: A Step-by-Step Treatment Manual,* ed. by D. H. Barlow (New York: Guilford Press, 2006); A. S. Filho, B. C. Maciel, M. M. Romano, T. F. Lascala, C. Trzesniak, M. C. Freitas-Ferrari, A. E. Nardi, R. Martín-Santos, A. W. Zuardi, and J. A. Crippa, "Mitral Valve Prolapse and Anxiety Disorders," *British Journal of Psychiatry: The Journal of Mental Science* 199, no. 3 (2011): 247–48.

8. R. Goldberg, "Clinical Presentations of Panic-Related Disorders," *Journal of Anxiety Disorders* 2, no. 1 (1988): 61–75.

9. Ibid; F. Veglio, F. Morello, S. Morra Di Cella, S. Del Colle, F. Rabbia, and P. Mulatero, "Recent Advances in Diagnosis and Treatment of Pheochromocytoma," *Minerva Medica* 94, no. 4 (2003): 267–71.

10. V. Hendrick, L. Altshuler, and P. Whybrow, "Psychoneuroendocrinology of Mood Disorders: The Hypothalamic-Pituitary-Thyroid Axis," *The Psychiatric Clinics of North America* 21, no. 2 (1998): 277–92.

11. E. A. Mayer, "Clinical Practice: Irritable Bowel Syndrome," *New England Journal of Medicine* 358, no. 16 (2008): 1692–99.

12. F. Lamers, P. van Oppen, H. C. Comijs, J. H. Smit, P. Spinhoven, A. J. van Balkom, W. A. Nolen, F. G. Zitman, A. T. Beekman, and B. W. Penninx, "Comorbidity Patterns of Anxiety and Depressive Disorders in a Large Cohort

Study: The Netherlands Study of Depression and Anxiety (NESDA)," *Journal of Clinical Psychiatry* 72, no. 3 (2011): 341–48.

13. R. C. Kessler, P. Berglund, O. Demler, R. Jin, D. Koretz, K. R. Merikangas, A. J. Rush, E. E. Walters, and P. S. Wang, "The Epidemiology of Major Depressive Disorder: Results from the National Comorbidity Survey Replication (NCS-R)," *Journal of the American Medical Association* 289, no. 23 (2003): 3095–105.

14. American Psychiatric Association, "Comorbidity of Depression and Generalized Anxiety Disorder," 2007, www.dsm5.org/research/pages/comor bidityofdepressionandgeneralizedanxietydisorder(june20-22,2007).aspx.

15. Ibid.

16. C. R. Spates, S. L. Pagoto, and A. Kalat, "A Qualitative and Quantitative Review of Behavioral Activation Treatment of Major Depressive Disorder," *Behavior Analyst Today* 7, no. 4 (2006): 508–21.

17. American Psychiatric Association, "DSM-5: The Future of Psychiatric Diagnosis," 2012, www.dsm5.org/Pages/Default.aspx.

18. L. Castle, R. E. Aubert, R. R. Verbrugge, M. Khalid, and R. S. Epstein, "Trends in Medication Treatment for ADHD," *Journal of Attention Disorders* 10, no. 4 (2007): 335–42; R. C. Kessler, L. Adler, R. Barkley, J. Biederman, C. K. Conners, O. Demler, S. V. Faraone, L. L. Greenhill, M. J. Howes, K. Secnik, T. Spencer, T. B. Ustün, E. E. Walters, and A. M. Zaslavsky, "The Prevalence and Correlates of Adult ADHD in the United States: Results from the National Comorbidity Survey Replication," *American Journal of Psychiatry* 163, no. 4 (2006): 716–23.

19. American Psychiatric Association, "DSM-5: The Future of Psychiatric Diagnosis," 2012. www.dsm5.org/Pages/Default.aspx.

20. R. C. Kessler, P. Berglund, O. Demler, R. Jin, K. R. Merikangas, and E. E. Walters, "Lifetime Prevalence and Age-of-Onset Distributions of DSM-IV Disorders in the National Comorbidity Survey Replication," *Archives of General Psychiatry* 62, no. 6 (2005): 593–602.

21. J. Swinbourne, C. Hunt, M. Abbott, J. Russell, T. St. Clare, and S. Touyz, "Comorbidity between Eating Disorders and Anxiety Disorders: Prevalence in an Eating Disorder Sample and Anxiety Disorder Sample," *Australian and New Zealand Journal of Psychiatry* 46, no. 2 (2012): 118–31; W. H. Kaye, C. M. Bulik, L. Thornton, N. Barbarich, and K. Masters, "Comorbidity of Anxiety Disorders with Anorexia and Bulimia Nervosa," *American Journal of Psychiatry* 161, no. 12 (2004): 2215–21.

22. E. P. Morris, S. H. Stewart, and L. S. Ham, "The Relationship between Social Anxiety Disorder and Alcohol Use Disorders: A Critical Review," *Clinical Psychology Review* 25, no. 6 (2005): 734–60; J. Robinson, J. Sareen, B. J. Cox, and J. M. Bolton, "Role of Self-Medication in the Development of Comorbid Anxiety and Substance Use Disorders: A Longitudinal Investigation," *Archives of General Psychiatry* 68, no. 8: 800–807.

23. R. Goldberg, "Clinical Presentations of Panic-Related Disorders," *Journal of Anxiety Disorders* 2 (1988): 61–75; H. C. Becker, "Alcohol Dependence, Withdrawal, and Relapse," *Alcohol Research and Health* 31, no. 4 (2008): 348–61.

24. Goldberg, "Clinical Presentations of Panic-Related Disorders," 61–75.

Chapter 4: What's Your Almost Anxious Flavor?

1. T. J. Meyer, M. L. Miller, R. L. Metzger, and T. D. Borkovec, "Development and Validation of the Penn State Worry Questionnaire," *Behavior Research and Therapy* 28, no. 6 (1990): 487–95.

2. K. M. Connor, J. R. Davidson, L. E. Churchill, A. Sherwood, E. Foa, and R. H. Weisler, "Psychometric Properties of the Social Phobia Inventory (SPIN). New Self-Rating Scale," *British Journal of Psychiatry: Journal of Mental Science* 176 (2000): 379–86.

3. Ibid; Z. Sosic, U. Gieler, and U. Stangier, "Screening for Social Phobia in Medical In- and Outpatients with the German Version of the Social Phobia Inventory (SPIN)," *Journal of Anxiety Disorders* 22, no. 5 (2008): 849–59; J. T. Chen, C. C. Lin, S. C. Wang, S. C. Liao, J. Y. Chen, C. Y. Liu, and M. B. Lee, "Finding Social Phobia Patients from the Internet," *Psychiatry Research* 190, no. 1 (2011): 121–25; F. L. Osório, J. A. Crippa, and S. R. Loureiro, "Evaluation of the Psychometric Properties of the Social Phobia Inventory in University Students," *Comprehensive Psychiatry* 51, no. 6 (2010): 630–40.

4. A. S. Zigmond and R. P. Snaith, "The Hospital Anxiety and Depression Scale," *Acta Psychiatrica Scandinavica* 67 (1983): 361–70.

5. I. Bjelland, A. A. Dahl, T. T. Haug, and D. Neckelmann, "The validity of the Hospital Anxiety and Depression Scale: An updated literature review," *Journal of Psychosomatic Research* 52 (2002): 69–77.

Chapter 5: Step Off the Almost Anxious Hamster Wheel

1. R. M. Rapee and R. G. Heimberg, "A Cognitive-Behavioral Model of Anxiety in Social Phobia," *Behaviour Research and Therapy* 35, no. 8 (1997): 741–56.

2. T. D. Borkovec, O. M. Alcaine, and E. Behar, "Avoidance Theory of Worry and Generalized Anxiety Disorder," in *Generalized Anxiety Disorder: Advances in Research and Practice*, ed. by R. G. Heimberg, C. L. Turk, and D. S. Mennin (New York: Guilford Press, 2006), 77–108.

3. D. M. Clark, "A Cognitive Approach to Panic," *Behaviour Research and Therapy* 24, no. 4 (1986): 461–70.

4. S. Taylor, W. J. Koch, and R. J. McNally, "How Does Anxiety Sensitivity Vary across the Anxiety Disorders?" *Journal of Anxiety Disorders* 6, no. 3 (1992): 249–59; S. Reiss, R. A. Peterson, D. M. Gursky, and R. J. McNally, "Anxiety Sensitivity, Anxiety Frequency and the Prediction of Fearfulness," *Behaviour Research and Therapy* 24, no. 1 (1986): 1–8.

Chapter 6: Anxiety or Avoidance: Focus on the True Enemy

1. A. Wells, D. M. Clark, P. M. Salkovskis, J. Ludgate, A. Hackmann, and M. G. Gelder, "Social Phobia: The Role of In-Situation Safety Behaviors in Maintaining Anxiety and Negative Beliefs," *Behavior Therapy* 26 (1995): 153–61; P. M. Salkovskis, D. M. Clark, and M. G. Gelder, "Cognition-Behaviour Links in the Persistence of Panic," *Behaviour Research and Therapy* 34, no. 5–6 (1996): 453–58.

2. D. M. Clark, "Anxiety Disorders: Why They Persist and How to Treat Them," *Behaviour Research and Therapy* 37, suppl. 1 (1999): S5–27.

3. E. Moitra, J. D. Herbert, and E. M. Forman, "Behavioral Avoidance Mediates the Relationship between Anxiety and Depressive Symptoms among Social Anxiety Disorder Patients," *Journal of Anxiety Disorders* 22, no. 7 (2008): 1205–13.

4. J. L. Trew, "Exploring the Roles of Approach and Avoidance in Depression: An Integrative Model," *Clinical Psychology Review* 31, no. 7 (2011): 1156–68.

5. B. J. Cox, G. R. Norton, R. P. Swinson, and N. S. Endler, "Substance Abuse and Panic- Related Anxiety: A Critical Review," *Behaviour Research and Therapy* 28, no. 5 (1990): 385–93.

Chapter 7: Let's Get Physical!

1. R. Walsh, "Lifestyle and Mental Health," *The American Psychologist* 66, no. 7 (2011): 579–92; D. A. Zellner, S. Loaiza, Z. Gonzalez, J. Pita, J. Morales, D. Pecora, and A. Wolf, "Food Selection Changes under Stress," *Physiology and Behavior* 87, no. 4 (2006): 789–93; L. M. Groesz, S. McCoy, J. Carl, L. Saslow, J. Stewart, N. Adler, B. Laraia, and E. Epel, "What Is Eating You? Stress and the Drive to Eat," *Appetite* 58, no. 2 (2012): 717–21.

2. H. J. Ramsawh, M. B. Stein, S. L. Belik, F. Jacobi, and J. Sareen, "Relationship of Anxiety Disorders, Sleep Quality, and Functional Impairment in a Community Sample," *Journal of Psychiatric Research* 43, no. 10 (2009): 926–33; M. Jansson-Fröjmark and K. Lindblom, "A Bidirectional Relationship between Anxiety and Depression, and Insomnia? A Prospective Study in the General Population," *Journal of Psychosomatic Research* 64, no. 4 (2008): 443–49; M. H. De Moor, A. L. Beem, J. H. Stubbe, D. I. Boomsma, and E. J. De Geus, "Regular Exercise, Anxiety, Depression and Personality: A Population-Based Study," *Preventive Medicine* 42, no. 4 (2006): 273–79.

3. Jansson-Fröjmark and Lindblom, "A Bidirectional Relationship between Anxiety and Depression, and Insomnia?" 443–49.

4. E. Epel, S. Jimenez, K. Brownell, L. Stroud, C. Stoney, and R. Niaura, "Are Stress Eaters at Risk for the Metabolic Syndrome?" *Annals of the New York Academy of Sciences* 1032 (2004): 208–10.

5. American Diabetes Association, "Standards of Medical Care in Diabetes—2009," *Diabetes Care* 32, suppl. 1 (2009): S13–S61.

6. N. Hermanns, T. Kubiak, B. Kulzer, and T. Haak, "Emotional Changes during Experimentally Induced Hypoglycaemia in Type 1 Diabetes," *Biological Psychology* 63, no. 1 (2003): 15–44.

7. R. E. Warren and B. M. Frier, "Hypoglycaemia and Cognitive Function," *Diabetes, Obesity and Metabolism* 7 no. 5 (2005): 493–503.

8. A. Keski-Rahkonen, J. Kaprio, A. Rissanen, M. Virkkunen, and R. J. Rose, "Breakfast Skipping and Health-Compromising Behaviors in Adolescents and Adults," *European Journal of Clinical Nutrition* 57, no. 7 (2003): 842–53.

9. B. J. Kaplan, S. G. Crawford, C. J. Field, and J. S. Simpson, "Vitamins, Minerals, and Mood," *Psychological Bulletin* 133, no. 5 (2007): 747–60; Walsh, "Lifestyle and Mental Health," 579–92.

10. K. R. Conner, M. Pinquart, and S. A. Gamble. "Meta-Analysis of Depression and Substance Use among Individuals with Alcohol Use Disorders," *Journal of Substance Abuse Treatment* 37, no. 2 (2009): 127–37; T. Roehrs and T. Roth, "Sleep, Sleepiness, and Alcohol Use," *Alcohol Research and Health* 25, no. 2 (2001): 101–109.

11. M. G. Kushner, K. Abrams, and C. Borchardt, "The Relationship between Anxiety Disorders and Alcohol Use Disorders: A Review of Major Perspectives and Findings," *Clinical Psychology Review* 20, no. 2 (2000): 149–71.

12. Jansson-Fröjmark and Lindblom, "A Bidirectional Relationship between Anxiety and Depression, and Insomnia?" 443–49; J. G. van Mill, W. J. Hoogendijk, N. Vogelzangs, R. van Dyck, and B. W. Penninx, "Insomnia and Sleep Duration in a Large Cohort of Patients with Major Depressive Disorder and Anxiety Disorders," *Journal of Clinical Psychiatry* 71, no. 3 (2010): 239–46.

13. M. Takahashi, "The Role of Prescribed Napping in Sleep Medicine," *Sleep Medicine Reviews* 7, no. 3 (2003): 227–35.

14. M. P. Herring, M. L. Jacob, C. Suveg, R. K. Dishman, and P. J. O'Connor, "Feasibility of Exercise Training for the Short-Term Treatment of Generalized Anxiety Disorder: A Randomized Controlled Trial," *Psychotherapy and Psychosomatics* 81, no. 1 (2012): 21–28.

15. M. P. Herring, P. J. O'Connor, and R. K. Dishman, "The Effect of Exercise Training on Anxiety Symptoms among Patients: A Systematic Review," *Archives of Internal Medicine* 170, no. 4 (2010): 321–31.

16. U.S. Department of Health and Human Services, "The Surgeon General's Vision for a Healthy and Fit Nation," 2010, www.surgeongeneral.gov/initiatives/healthy-fit- nation/obesityvision2010.pdf.

Chapter 8: Tapping Into the Power of Your Social Network

1. P. K. Maulik, W. W. Eaton, and C. P. Bradshaw, "The Effect of Social Networks and Social Support on Common Mental Disorders Following Specific Life Events," *Acta Psychiatrica Scandinavica* 122, no. 2 (2010): 118–28; R. B. Flannergy Jr. and D. Wieman, "Social Support, Life Stress, and Psychological Distress: An Empirical Assessment," *Journal of Clinical Psychology* 45, no. 6 (1989): 867–72.

2. L. M. Heinrich and E. Gullone, "The Clinical Significance of Loneliness: A Literature Review," *Clinical Psychology Review* 26, no. 6 (2006): 695–718; S. Nolen-Hoeksema and C. Ahrens, "Age Differences and Similarities in the Correlates of Depressive Symptoms," *Psychology and Aging* 17, no. 1 (2002): 116–24; J. T. Cacioppo, L. C. Hawkley, L. E. Crawford, J. M. Ernst, M. H. Burleson, R. B. Kowalewski, W. B. Malarkey, E. Van Cauter, and G. G. Berntson, "Loneliness and Health: Potential Mechanisms," *Psychosomatic Medicine* 64, no. 3 (2002): 407–17.

3. Maulik, Eaton, and Bradshaw, "Effect of Social Networks and Social Support," 118–28.

4. M. A. Whisman, C. Sheldon, and P. Goering, "Psychiatric Disorders and Dissatisfaction with Social Relationships: Does Type of Relationship Matter?" *Journal of Abnormal Psychology* 109, no. 4 (2000): 803–8.

5. C. A. Langston, "Capitalizing on and Coping with Daily Life Events: Expressive Responses to Positive Events," *Journal of Personality and Social Psychology* 67, no. 6 (1994): 1112–25.

6. S. L. Gable, G. C. Gonzaga, and A. Strachman, "Will You Be There for Me When Things Go Right? Supportive Responses to Positive Event Disclosures," *Journal of Personality and Social Psychology* 91, no. 5 (2006): 904–17.

7. J. T. Cacioppo, J. H. Fowler, and N. A. Christakis, "Alone in the Crowd: The Structure and Spread of Loneliness in a Large Social Network," *Journal of Personality and Social Psychology* 97, no. 6 (2009): 977–91.

8. J. H. Fowler and N. A. Christakis, "Dynamic Spread of Happiness in a Large Social Network: Longitudinal Analysis over 20 Years in the Framingham Heart Study," *British Medical Journal* 337 (2008): a2338; N. A. Christakis and J. H. Fowler, "The Collective Dynamics of Smoking in a Large Social Network," *New England Journal of Medicine* 358, no. 21 (2008): 2249–58; N.A. Christakis and J. H Fowler, "The Spread of Obesity in a Large Social Network over 32 Years," *New England Journal of Medicine* 357, no. 4 (2007): 370–79.

9. G. D. Zimet, N. W. Dahlem, S. G. Zimet, and K. G. Farley, "The Multidimensional Scale of Perceived Social Support," *Journal of Personality Assessment* 52, no. 1 (1988): 30–41.

10. I. P. Clara, B. J. Cox, M. W. Enns, L. T. Murray, and L. J. Torgrud, "Confirmatory Factor Analysis of the Multidimensional Scale of Perceived Social Support in Clinically Distressed and Student Samples," *Journal of Personality Assessment* 81, no. 3 (2003): 265–70; V. Cicero, G. Lo Coco, S. Gullo, and G. Lo Verso, "The Role of Attachment Dimensions and Perceived Social Support in Predicting Adjustment to Cancer," *Psycho-Oncology* 18, no. 10 (2009): 1045–52; L. J. Torgrud, J. R. Walker, L. Murray, B. J. Cox, M. Chartier, and K. D. Kjernisted, "Deficits in Perceived Social Support Associated with Generalized Social Phobia," *Cognitive Behaviour Therapy* 33, no. 2 (2004): 87–96.

11. Clara et al., "Confirmatory Factor Analysis of the Multidimensional Scale of Perceived Social Support," 265–70.

12. Ibid.

13. Cicero et al., "The Role of Attachment Dimensions and Perceived Social Support," 1045–52.

14. Torgrud et al., "Deficits in Perceived Social Support," 87–96.

15. D. Vandervoort, "Quality of Social Support in Mental and Physical Health," *Current Psychology* 18, no. 2 (1999): 205–22.

Chapter 10: It's Time to Feel Comfortably Uncomfortable

1. B. J. Deacon and J. S. Abramowitz, "Cognitive and Behavioral Treatments for Anxiety Disorders: A Review of Meta-Analytic Findings," *Journal of Clinical Psychology* 60, no. 4 (2004) 429–41; P. J. Norton and E. C. Price, "A Meta-Analytic Review of Adult Cognitive- Behavioral Treatment Outcome across the Anxiety Disorders," *Journal of Nervous and Mental Disease* 195, no. 6 (2007): 521–31.

2. P. L. Anderson, E. Zimand, L. F. Hodges, and B. O. Rothbaum, "Cognitive Behavioral Therapy for Public-Speaking Anxiety Using Virtual Reality for Exposure," *Depression and Anxiety* 22, no. 3 (2005): 156–58.

3. M. B. Powers and P. M. G. Emmelkamp, "Virtual Reality Exposure Therapy for Anxiety Disorders: A Meta-Analysis," *Journal of Anxiety Disorders* 22, no. 3 (2008): 561–69.

4. F. H. Wilhelm and W. T. Roth, "Acute and Delayed Effects of Alprazolam on Flight Phobics during Exposure," *Behaviour Research and Therapy* 35, no. 9 (1997): 831–41; I. M. Marks, R. P. Swinson, M. Basoğlu, K. Kuch, H. Noshirvani, G. O'Sullivan, P. T. Lelliott, M. Kirby, G. McNamee, S. Sengun, et al., "Alprazolam and Exposure Alone and Combined in Panic Disorder with Agoraphobia. A Controlled Study in London and Toronto," *British Journal of Psychiatry* 162 (1993): 776–87; H. A. Westra and S. H. Stewart, "Cognitive Behavioural Therapy and Pharmacotherapy: Complementary or Contradictory Approaches to the Treatment of Anxiety?" *Clinical Psychology Review* 18, no. 3 (1998): 307–40.

5. T. Sloan and M. J. Telch, "The Effects of Safety-Seeking Behavior and Guided Threat Reappraisal on Fear Reduction during Exposure: An Experimental Investigation," *Behaviour Research and Therapy* 40, no. 3 (2002): 235–51; K. Beesdo-Baum, E. Jenjahn, M. Höfler, U. Lueken, E. S. Becker, and J. Hoyer, "Avoidance, Safety Behavior, and Reassurance Seeking in Generalized Anxiety Disorder," *Depression and Anxiety* 29, no. 11 (2012): 948–57.

Chapter 11: Be Here Now

1. J. Kabat-Zinn, *Wherever You Go, There You Are: Mindfulness Meditation in Everyday Life* (New York: Hyperion, 1994).

2. L. L. Bowman, L. E. Levine, B. M. Waite, and M. Gendron, "Can Students Really Multitask? An Experimental Study of Instant Messaging While Reading," *Computers and Education* 54, no. 4 (2010): 927–31.

3. S. Evans, S. Ferrando, M. Findler, C. Stowell, C. Smart, and D. Haglin, "Mindfulness- Based Cognitive Therapy for Generalized Anxiety Disorder," *Journal of Anxiety Disorders* 22, no. 4 (2008): 716–21; S. G. Hofmann, A. T. Sawyer, A. A. Witt, and D. Oh, "The Effect of Mindfulness-Based Therapy on Anxiety and Depression: A Meta-Analytic Review," *Journal of Consulting and Clinical Psychology* 78, no. 2 (2010): 169–83; L. Roemer, S. M. Orsillo, and K. Salters-Pedneault, "Efficacy of an Acceptance-Based Behavior Therapy for Generalized Anxiety Disorder: Evaluation in a Randomized Controlled Trial," *Journal of Consulting and Clinical Psychology* 76, no. 6 (2008): 1083–89; J. Simpson and T. Mapel, "An Investigation into the Health Benefits of Mindfulness-Based Stress Reduction (MBSR) for People Living with a Range of Chronic Physical Illnesses in New Zealand," *New Zealand Medical Journal* 124, no. 1338 (2011): 68–75; S. Rosenzweig, J. M. Greeson, D. K. Reibel, J. S. Green, S. A. Jasser, and D. Beasley, "Mindfulness-Based Stress Reduction for Chronic Pain Conditions: Variation in Treatment Outcomes and Role of Home Meditation Practice," *Journal of Psychosomatic Research* 68, no. 1 (2010): 29–36; Bowman et al., "Can Students Really Multitask?" 927–31; R. G. Wanden-Berghe, J. Sanz-Valero, C. Wanden-Berghe, "The Application of Mindfulness to Eating Disorders Treatment: A Systematic Review," *Eating Disorders* 19, no. 1 (2011): 34–48; K. Birnie, S. N. Garland, and L. E. Carlson, "Psychological Benefits for Cancer Patients and Their Partners Participating in Mindfulness-Based Stress Reduction (MBSR)," *Psychooncology* 19, no. 9 (2010): 1004–1009.

4. Hofmann et al., "The Effect of Mindfulness-Based Therapy on Anxiety and Depression," 169–83.

5. R. Davidson, "Alterations in Brain and Immune Function Produced by Mindfulness Meditation," *Psychosomatic Medicine* 65, no. 4 (2003): 564–70.

6. L. A. Kilpatrick, B. Y. Suyenobu, S. R. Smith, J. A. Bueller, T. Goodman, J. D. Creswell, K.Tillisch, E. A. Mayer, and B. D. Naliboff, "Impact of Mindfulness-Based Stress Reduction Training on Intrinsic Brain Connectivity," *NeuroImage* 56, no. 1 (2011): 290–98.

7. B. K. Hölzel, J. Carmody, M. Vangel, C. Congleton, S. M. Yerramsetti, T. Gard, and S. W. Lazar, "Mindfulness Practice Leads to Increases in Regional Brain Gray Matter Density," *Psychiatry Research: Neuroimaging* 191, no. 1 (2011): 36–43.

Chapter 12: When You Need More Tools in Your Kit

1. L. Marques, N. J. LeBlanc, H. M. Weingarden, K. R. Timpano, M. Jenike, and S. Wilhelm, "Barriers to Treatment and Service Utilization in an Internet Sample of Individuals with Obsessive-Compulsive Symptoms," *Depression and Anxiety* 27, no. 5 (2010): 470–75; M. Chartier-Otis, M. Perreault, and C. Bélanger, "Determinants of Barriers to Treatment for Anxiety Disorders," *Psychiatric Quarterly* 81, no. 2 (2010): 127–38.

2. M. W. Otto, R. K. McHugh, and K. M. Kantak, "Combined Pharmacotherapy and Cognitive-Behavioral Therapy for Anxiety Disorders: Medication Effects, Glucocorticoids, and Attenuated Treatment Outcomes," *Clinical Psychology: Science and Practice* 17, no. 2 (2010): 91–103.

3. S. E. Lakhan and K. F. Vieira, "Nutritional and Herbal Supplements for Anxiety and Anxiety-Related Disorders: Systematic Review," *Nutrition Journal* 9, no. 1 (2010): 42; G. Kinrys, E. Coleman, and E. Rothstein, "Natural Remedies for Anxiety Disorders: Potential Use and Clinical Applications," *Depression and Anxiety* 26, no. 3 (2009): 259–65.

4. K. Linde, G. Ramirez, C. D. Mulrow, A. Pauls, W. Weidenhammer, and D. Melchart, "St John's Wort for Depression—An Overview and Meta-Analysis of Randomised Clinical Trials," *British Medical Journal* 313, no. 7052 (1996): 253–58; K. A. Kobak, L. V. Taylor, R. Futterer, and G. Warner, "St. John's Wort in Generalized Anxiety Disorder: Three More Case Reports," *Journal of Clinical Psychopharmacology* 23, no. 5 (2003): 531–32; J. R. Davidson and K. M. Connor, "St. John's Wort in Generalized Anxiety Disorder: Three Case Reports," *Journal of Clinical Psychopharmacology* 21, no. 6 (2001): 635–36; K. A. Kobak, L. V. Taylor, G. Warner, and R. Futterer, "St. John's Wort versus Placebo in Social Phobia: Results from a Placebo- Controlled Pilot Study," *Journal of Clinical Psychopharmacology* 25, no. 1 (2005): 51–58.

5. Lakhan and Vieira, "Nutritional and Herbal Supplements for Anxiety and Anxiety-Related Disorders," 42; Kinrys, Coleman, and Rothstein, "Natural Remedies for Anxiety Disorders," 259–65; U.S. Food and Drug Administration, "Consumer Advisory: Kava-Containing Dietary Supplements May Be Associated with Severe Liver Injury," 2002, www.fda.gov/Food/ResourcesForYou/Consumers/ucm085482.htm.

6. Kinrys, Coleman, and Rothstein, "Natural Remedies for Anxiety Disorders," 259–65.

7. Ibid.

8. Lakhan and Vieira, "Nutritional and Herbal Supplements for Anxiety and Anxiety-Related Disorders," 42.

Chapter 13: Practicing Skills for a Lifetime

1. P. C. Kendall, B. Chu, A. Gifford, C. Hayes, M. Nauta, "Breathing Life into a Manual: Flexibility and Creativity with Manual-Based Treatments," *Cognitive and Behavioral Practice* 5, no. 2 (1998): 177–98.

about the authors

Luana Marques, PhD, is an assistant professor of psychology at Harvard Medical School, the director of psychotherapy research and training at Massachusetts General Hospital and Harvard Medical School, and the director of the Hispanic Clinical Research Program at Massachusetts General Hospital and Harvard Medical School. Her groundbreaking research focuses on the presentation and treatment of anxiety disorders, with a particular focus on cultural differences in the phenomenology of anxiety as well as the dissemination and implementation of empirically supported treatments for anxiety to minority populations. Her research has been funded by the National Institute of Mental Health and the Multicultural Affairs Office at the Massachusetts General Hospital. She has published more than thirty articles and chapters, has served as the program chair of the Anxiety and Depression Association of America (ADAA), and is a member of the American Psychological Association (APA) and the Association for Behavioral Cognitive Therapies (ABCT). She is also actively involved in training and supervising clinical psychology interns at Massachusetts General Hospital. Dr. Marques maintains a private psychotherapy practice in Boston, where she treats individuals with almost anxiety, clinical anxiety, and mood disorders. Connect with her online at www.luanamarquesphd.com or follow her on Twitter at @drluanamarques.

Eric Metcalf, MPH, is a writer and health communicator based in Indianapolis. He has coauthored or contributed to more than a dozen books on health and fitness and written widely for magazines and online publications. He's also a producer and contributor for the weekly *Sound Medicine* public radio program.

∎ ◆ ∎

Hazelden, a national nonprofit organization founded in 1949, helps people reclaim their lives from the disease of addiction. Built on decades of knowledge and experience, Hazelden offers a comprehensive approach to addiction that addresses the full range of patient, family, and professional needs, including treatment and continuing care for youth and adults, research, higher learning, public education and advocacy, and publishing.

A life of recovery is lived "one day at a time." Hazelden publications, both educational and inspirational, support and strengthen lifelong recovery. In 1954, Hazelden published *Twenty-Four Hours a Day,* the first daily meditation book for recovering alcoholics, and Hazelden continues to publish works to inspire and guide individuals in treatment and recovery, and their loved ones. Professionals who work to prevent and treat addiction also turn to Hazelden for evidence-based curricula, informational materials, and videos for use in schools, treatment programs, and correctional programs.

Through published works, Hazelden extends the reach of hope, encouragement, help, and support to individuals, families, and communities affected by addiction and related issues.

For questions about Hazelden publications,
please call **800-328-9000** or visit us online
at **hazelden.org/bookstore.**

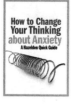